D1241319

Wealth

of

Wisdom

Maxine Spyres Hixon

Wealth

of

Wisdom

Maxine Spyres Hixon

Copyright © 2016
All Rights Reserved

PUBLISHED BY:
BRENTWOOD CHRISTIAN PRESS
P. O. BOX 4773
COLUMBUS, GEORGIA 31914-4773
(800) 334-8861
WWW.BRENTWOODBOOKS.COM

"If any of you lack wisdom, let him ask of God, who giveth to all men liberally, and upbraideth not, and it shall be given him."

—James 1:5

Foreword

As prolific as Maxine was, one would think she didn't do anything other than write poetry, but the opposite was true! Maxine was a busy housewife – she sang gospel songs on her minister husband, Carl's, Missionary Baptist radio broadcast for over fifty years. She played the piano well, practicing everyday, except on Sundays. She was absolutely the best cook in the world, to which her family can attest. She sewed, and crocheted to perfection, many afghans, shawls and dainty doilies, and she painted. Many of her paintings hang in the house she and Carl had custom-built, and of which she designed. Besides all this, she was a real estate broker. She had fun making cheese and soap. In her own words she said, "There are so many things I like to do!" She possessed a real joy in living, and, ever since we were kids, we remember her singing in the kitchen, as she went about her daily tasks.

Maxine was like the woman of Proverbs, chapter 31, of whom could be said, "…her children all arise and call her blessed!" Her volumes of poetry leave behind a lasting legacy. Her collections can be found on the shelves of the top fifty colleges and universities in the United States, and in all the Nursing Homes throughout Arkansas. She always held a special place in her heart for the elderly.

Maxine loved lost souls dearly and won many souls to Jesus. The Bible says, "He that winneth souls is wise, and shall shine as the stars of the firmament."

Dad's preaching and Mother's teaching won all of us kids to Christ at an early age, and we are looking forward to seeing them again in Heaven, as she says in one of her poems "…when it comes our time to view life's setting of the sun." In speaking to her husband, in one of her poems, concerning leading us kids to Christ, she said, "In that, we failed not," and she goes on to say, "Hell will be so very hot." So if you do not know Jesus as your personal Saviour, may you accept Him now. Although many souls were won during her lifetime, the fruits of her labors, the Bible says, can still follow after.

Wealth of Wisdom promises "a good read," so enjoy it! May your receive a special blessing!

Affectionately,

Maxine's two daughters,
Tena M. Hixon and Pamela Hixon Rhea

Biography

Maxine Spyres was born on January 29, 1926, in Adair County, Stilwell, Oklahoma.

She was valedictorian of her eighth grade class, and finished high school a year early. She married Carl W. Hixon on October 6, 1945 in Selma, California. They have four children: Tena, Pamela, Ronald, and Rodney.

Maxine attended the Northeastern State Teacher's College in Tahlequah, Oklahoma. She taught school during World War II in a one-room schoolhouse – children of all ages.

Maxine's collection of inspirational poetry published in recent years are *Sand and Pearls, Voice of the Heart, Mither,* (a collection of one hundred twenty-two poems, written in its entirety after Maxine suffered a left-side paralysis stroke,) *Poetic Potpourri, Hidden Treasure (Volumes 1 and 11, & 111,)* and this volume, *Wealth of Wisdom.* In 1995, Maxine collaborated with her two daughters, to write a children's book, *Rhymes of the Time* published in 2015, which she illustrated.

Maxine's poems have been published in their hometown *Log Cabin Democrat* for over forty-eight years, and continue to be printed each Sunday. Many of her poems have won prizes in poetry contests, been published in anthologies, and are on the Internet.

Maxine and her family made their home in Conway, Arkansas, for over thirty-eight years, where her two daughters continue to reside.

This volume, *Wealth of Wisdom,* completes seven volumes of inspirational and religious poetry, not including the children's rhyme book, and the book, *Mither,* written after having a stroke. Maxine passed from this life on, December 2, 2006, exactly seven months and seven days after suffering a massive stroke. Her daughters have published her works posthumously.

Her works will continue to live on in the hearts and minds of her many readers, whose lives will be made richer for the reading.

Poetry Collections by Maxine:

Sand and Pearls
Voice of the Heart
Poetic Potpourri
Mither
Rhymes of the Time (children's book — a collaboration
with her daughters)
Hidden Treasure I
Hidden Treasure II
Hidden Treasure III

Table of Contents

SALVATION

The Only Way...21
God's Great Power 22
You Must Choose 24
What is it Then? 24
Work to Do 26
Forgive Us, Lord (Villanelle) 27
God's Love Never Fails 28

HEAVEN and HELL

Time is Wasting (Villanelle).....................................31
God's River..32
It's Up To You..33
It's Your Choice 34
After the Grave 34
The devil..35

COMFORT, HOPE and INSPIRATION

Faith 39
Faith Delivers 40
Faith (Think and Dream) 41
Faith is the Substance 42
Only Believe..43
"I Love Thee, Lord" 44
Who Are We? 45

Only One Good 46
Mercy 47
God's Will or Mine! 48
Lighting the Way 49
Tunnel of Life..50
A Nice Surprise 51
Patience 51
Compassion 52
In a Crowd 53
"Speak Up"..54
Choices While Decision 54
Let God Fight For You 55
Go With What You Know...56
Living Now...57
Be Very Strong 58
Give or Take 59
Character Counts (Skeltonic Verse) 60
Not a Village! But Parents 61
Steady On 62
Delight in the Lord 63
Somber Thoughts 65
Sadness..66
So Much Trouble!..67
Looking Up Only in Affliction! 67
Misunderstood 68
Along Life's Way 69
Light in the Dark 71
Don't Wait Too Late 72
So Thankful He Cares 73
Friends 74
Someone Besides 76
"Lord, Help Me"...77
"Dear Lord, Help Us All"..78
Calm Midst the Storm 79
Real Comfort 80
At Peace 81
There's a Reason 82
The Past 83

Can't Change the Past 84
"Now" – Between the Past and Future....................................85
The Future 86
Time Doesn't Change Everything 87
Even in Changed Circumstances 88
Ode on Happiness..89
True Happiness..90
Keep Looking Up! 91

SEASONAL and OCCASIONAL

Thank God for the Pilgrims (Triolet) 95
Christmas Tree 95
The Heart Can Still Know Though the Tinsel Goes................97
Bells of Christmas 98
Love 98
Whose Birthday? (Cinquain) 99
Now's the Time 99
Retreat or Advance 100
The Newborn King 101
What Gifts For Christ? 102
Lest We Forget..103
An Old Remedy..104
Another Year??? 105
Spent, But Not Gone 106
Valentine's Mine 107
Today and Always 108
Valentine, It Matters Not (Triolet).......................................109
The Meaning of Easter "Come Ye" 110
The Meaning of Easter (Triolet) 111
The Fourth of July (Triolet)..111
Father's Day 112

NATURE

Beauty Here ... More Beauty Hereafter (Villanelle)...............115
The Apple 116

The Winter's Moon (Rondeau) 117
Fog...118
Waiting 119
Waiting for Spring 120
How Does Your Garden Grow?...121
Night and Day (Sestina) 123
We Wait, But, the Roses Won't (A Ghazal)...............................125
Beneath the Surface..127
Quiet 128
Softly 129
Busy, Busy, Busy! 130
The Butterfly 131
Summertime 133
But, the Calendar and Almanac? 135
Earth's Sounds...136
In Time (Gardening) 137

DOCTRINAL and DIDACTIC

Courage 141
Forgiveness 142
Reaping What You Sow...143
Have Unstaggering Faith..144
Did You Know? 146
Grow Up!...147
Or Would You Rather Be a Pig?!..148
What If?..149
Are You Ready?..151
Death 152
The Heart of Things 153
Determination is Rife! 155
Old is Forever New! 157
God Knew Us Before and After 158
The Lord's Church...159
Gifts of God –Not Man 160

CINQUAINS, HAIKU, SENRYU, LUNES, SONNETS AND TRIOLETS

Something New (Triolet)...165
No Place to Hide (Triolet) 165
It's Priorities, Stupid!(Triolet) 166
True Values 166
Forever Young (Triolet)..167
Fragile? Think Again (Triolet) 167
Our Daughter (Triolet) 168
So Many Things (Triolet) 168
Memory Lane (Sonnet) 169
Upheld (Sonnet) 169
A Fortunate Situation (Cinquain) 170
A Different Name (Cinquain) 170
End of School (Triolet) 170
Which? (Senryu) 171
Father's Day (Triolet) 171
You Never Knew Until Now (Triolet)...171
Dreamed? (Cinquain) 172
Sight-seeing (Cinquain)...172
Repeat (Cinquain) 172
Together (Cinquain) 173
Love in Action (Cinquain)..173
In Its Own Time (Cinquain) 173
Vengeance Belongs to God (Cinquain) 174
Forward March (Cinquain) 174
A Long Wait (Cinquain) 174
Above Par (Cinquain) 175
Mother's Day (Triolet) 175
No Time (Triolet) 175
Haiku – hurry..176
God So Loved (Triolet) 176
By Grace Through Faith (Triolet)...176
The Summer Sun (Triolet)..177
The Evergreen (Triolet)..177
The Red Rose (Triolet) 178
Parents Are Responsible (Triolet) 178

Lies (Triolet) 179

Difference in Work and Play (Triolet)....................179

To Write a Sonnet (Sonnet) 180

Same, Same (Triolet)...180

West Texas (Cinquain)...181

I Remember (Cinquain)..181

One or More! (Cinquain)...181

Work Fast (Cinquain) 182

In Order (Cinquain)..182

It's Gold (Cinquain)..182

Quiet When Busy (Cinquain) 183

Haiku – night sky 183

Haiku – a poem! 183

Senryu –The crow ... .183

On Writing (Triolet) 184

Senryu – A large inheritance ... .184

Cart Before the Horse (Cinquain) 184

Senryu – Small package 185

Reaches Far (Cinquain)...185

God's Will (Cinquain) 185

God's Love Turning to Hate (Cinquain) 185

In God's Care (Cinquain) 186

God's Perspective (Cinquain) 186

Dead End (Cinquain)..186

Keeping Time (Cinquain) 187

Magnified (Cinquain) 187

On the Lord's Side (Cinquain) 187

Faith (Cinquain) 188

God's Will (Cinquain) 188

God's Way (Cinquain) 188

Rest to Work (Cinquain) 189

Faith (Cinquain) 189

Senryu – A truck 189

Actions Louder Than Words! (Cinquain) 190

Senryu – Pristine white 190

Senryu – Diamond encrusted 190

Senryu – Most weddings 190

Useless (Cinquain) 191
14

Senryu – Rain clouds today.....................................191
Senryu – Bad mood 191
Senryu – Be careful 191
Haiku – sleet, ice, snow...192
Life (Cinquain) 192
Lune – salvation's through Christ 192
Lune – though family loves you 192
Lune – birds have no lessons...................................193
Lune – in kitchen all day 193
Senryu – Some people's faults 193
Pick and Choose (Cinquain) 193
Haiku – hurry have fun 194
Just Cogitating! (Triolet)...194
The Real One Please Stand (Cinquain) 194
What's the Final Answer? (Triolet) 195
A Must (Cinquain)..195
Covetousness (Triolet)...195
Touch Not Mine Anointed (Triolet) 196
The Empty Tomb (Cinquain)....................................196
Christ Arose (Cinquain)..197
Lune – no rain … it's so dry 197
Lune – not hungry at all 197
Lune – sunshine during day......................................197
Senryu – Haircut 198
Senryu – A little boy 198
Senryu – Silk stockings 198
Senryu – Never know 198
Haiku – God's angels 199
Senryu – Telescope 199
Senryu – What goes 199
Senryu – Portrait artist...199
Haiku – earth's canopy 200
Haiku – picture perfect 200
Senryu – A horse of 200
Haiku – full moon 200
Senryu – Two armies 201
Senryu – Computer 201
Senryu – Piggy bank 201

Senryu – Removed 201
Senryu – Natural 202
Senryu – A pretty tune..202
Senryu – Labor Day?...202
Put No Confidence in the Flesh (Cinquain) 202
Quiet Strength (Cinquain) 203
Renewed Heart (Cinquain) 203
Passing the Test (Cinquain)..203
We Ask and Receive Not (Cinquain).....................................204
Power in Prayer (Cinquain)...204
Plunging Into Hell (Cinquain)..204
More Than a Life (Cinquain) 205
Jabez' Prayer 205
Jabez, God is My God 206
Senryu – The preacher...206
"Wild Green" Picking (Triolet) 206
The "Salt Box" House (Triolet)..207
On Hate (Triolet) 207
Despondency (Triolet)...208
The Way to God is Through His Son (Triolet) 208

ECLECTIC

Unusual 211
Have Your Ever? I Have 212
Level the Playing Field 214
Cats Kill Pests 215
I Was Thought of First! 215
All Mouth 216
A Dumb Animal? – Who Said? Not I! 216
Good-bye Big Fish 217
Losing Weight 218
The Mule 219
Thankless...220
Camouflage 221
One Thing Calls For Another 222
All To Himself ... Yet, Not Alone 224

Where My Money Went 225
"Gems" of Wisdom by Maxine 226
Logging a Log 227
Your Job and You (Sonnet) 228
Perspective's the Difference 229
The Mouse 230

NOSTALGIA and ROMANCE

To Catch a Snowbird 235
Time Has Told (Villanelle) 236
If It's True Love (Triolet) 237
True Love (Triolet) 237
Remembering Where We Met (Triolet).................................238
Without Price (Sonnet) 238
"Better Than Sunday" 239
New With the Old Versus Old With the New 240
The Three " R's" and More 242
Poverty and Wealth 244
Tell Me 245

HOME and FAMILY

Welcome!...249
Some Remain 251
All Not Said or Done...252
What's a Birthday? 253
Children Pay 255
Charity and Home 256
Shadow 257

Salvation

The Only Way

For God so loved the world, He gave His Son,
His only begotten; to set us free.
That whoever believeth in Him,
Should not perish, but have everlasting life.

Salvation's call is to "Whosoever …
Will: may come take of the water of life .
Freely" … secure in His love forever;
Even in the midst of turmoil and strife.

Twelve legions of angels; Christ could have called;
To deliver Him from death on the cross …
Where willingly He died, for you and me:
That all who believe, should never be lost.

By grace are we saved, through faith; not by works:
God's grace to man is, "unmerited favor" …
It's not of ourselves, lest any should boast;
Allegiance due, to a loving Saviour.

If Salvation could come another way …
Christ's death on the cross would have been in vain;
Yet, He gave His life, man's sin debt to pay;
That Hell might be shunned, with Heaven to gain.

Though man was made from the dust of the earth;
God created him with the power of choice …
Salvation is in Christ: through the New Birth;
Whosoever will … means man has a voice.

Eternal life's by repentance and faith …
Christ is Salvation's one and only door;
It's for whosoever … God's love is great;
His blessings include the rich and the poor.

Christ will never leave or forsake His own;
In life, many blessings, He has in store …
All who are saved will have a Heavenly Home;
All believers: now and those gone before.

Jesus is the way, the truth and the life:
Only way to the Father is through Him …
Works for Salvation; through the world is rife;
The devil is author of all of them.

God's Great Power

The firmament declareth the handiwork of God:
We can read this in God's Holy Word,
Many things surround us showing His greatness;
The tall mountains with the dogwood trees,
The rock formations in the foothills,
The lake in sight … placid and serene,
Flowers of all colors blooming midst grass so green,
The old oak tree with heavy limbs making a dense shade.
Birds in the trees singing their very own song,
The cool breeze softly blowing the leaves,
The spider weaving an intricate silver web,
The different color roses of perfection and long-stemmed
    grace.
Man, tired in body and mind, renewed by a night's rest;

The spirit of man revived from time spent in study and
    prayer,
Increased faith ... ready to accept what life offers,
In forgiveness, letting go of the bitter, caused by sin,
To be useful in the Master's service, for we were
    bought with a price.
Jesus died for all on the cross that we might
    have life and have it more abundantly.
Many people seem to think the wonders of the
    world only show God's greatness,
But, a soul transformed in Salvation shows God's
    power – the greatest of all –
A wayward soul on the road to Hell ... made
    ready through accepting Christ for a Heavenly home.
God does show His power in all that surrounds us,
Proving to man he is without excuse in rejecting
    God's Son,
Some can paint beautiful pictures after much painstaking
    work,
Or can build great magnificent buildings,
    bridges, roads, gardens and such,
If health permits, and God allows one's time
    to go on,
A lot of, "Ifs" can get in the way of the workings
    of man.
When God, in creation, spoke the world into existence
    and all things therein.
What is man, oh, Lord, that Thou art mindful of him?
Man was made in God's likeness – He gave His
    only begotten Son to die that man
        might have everlasting life through believing in Him.

You Must Choose

Trusting the Lord is best ...
Doing what we ought –.
God will take care of the rest.
On Calvary, our Salvation was bought.

We trust the Lord for
    care of our soul ...;
But, worry and fret ... with such regret –;
When happenings in life
    to our desire don't mold;
Christ cares for His own ...
    when we trust and let.

We're not our own ...
    we're bought with a price;
When we accept the Saviour as our own –
Repentance and faith for
    Salvation does suffice.
In unbelief and doubt ...
    one can worry until life is gone.

What is it Then?

Down through time, God's men have preached ...
The ones God called ... the lost to reach –;
Since Christ organized His Church on the shores of Galilee;
There've been faithful followers, preaching to help set
        souls free.

Preaching God's Word … telling of His saving grace.
Of how Jesus was sent to die for the human race –;
How He died on Calvary's rugged cross;
Saving all who would believe in Him … overcoming sin's
      dross.

The Apostle Paul made tents and, … preached …
Down through the ages others have worked, to be able to
      preach and teach;
The gifts and callings of God are without repentance –;
After a hard day's work… on God's Word, they took their
      stance.

Now, as we know it … this modern time …
It seems many choose to listen to stories or rhyme;
God's promise, the Holy Spirit will accompany HIS WORD;
To the convicting, of those who hear … or have heard.

What is it then … when multitudes come forward …
When scant, if any scripture is used to MAR their MODERN
      (gospel?)
To be saved, one must believe what Jesus taught while here on
      earth;
By grace through faith in Him is Salvation, or the New Birth.

As the tree falleth … so shall it lie …;
We are … as we are … when to earth we've said good-bye;
Today is the day of Salvation … now is the accepted time;
Though God is longsuffering, His love … with judgment is
      combined.

Salvation is by repentance and faith in Christ …;
When Christ died, He paid Salvation's price –;
People who wait for a, "great gathering" their faith to state;
Much publicity at any rate ... but, after death ... too late the
        state of
                The
                Soul
                To
                    Debate!!!

Work to Do

Christ said He came to do the Will,
Of His Father Who sent Him.
We should be willing to do our best,
Not what's accomplished – trying's the test.
    … God looks on the heart;
That's where He always starts.

In planting grain, the life is in the heart;
If the earth is good, new life comes forth.
Like produces like – always the same.
When we the Name of Christ proclaim;
We need be sincere – excuses, lame.
Life is much more than just a game.

As Christ did His work while here on earth
Coming to die, paying the price – our New Birth.
It's for everyone ... you and me.
So thankful we all should be.
After accepting Him we need do His Will;
While life on earth, allowed us still.

What time we spend, here below,
Should not be spent, just for show.
... busy doing our Lord's work;
We should obey and never shirk.
For us, He has gone to prepare a mansion;
All who are His will reach their Heavenly station!

"Forgive Us, Lord"

(Villanelle)

"Forgive us, Lord," we all should pray;
Though falling short ... missing the mark,
He protects us by night and day.

For unforgiven sins, we pay,
God's forgiveness is where to start;
"Forgive us, Lord," we all should pray;

We're born in sin; ... sin brings decay
Until God's Spirit does His part,
He protects us by night and day.

His power holds the devil at bay;
Convicts of sin as with a dart,
"Forgive us, Lord," we all should pray;

With Christ, there's peace through midst of life's fray,
Looks not on person, but the heart,
He protects us by night and day.

Come … Christ died for All! Any may:
For by grace are you saved through faith,
"Forgive us, Lord," we all should pray;
He protects us by night and day.

God's Love Never Fails

(Written Sept. 6, 1960)

In love, God sent His only Son,
To die on the cross.
To save the souls of sinners.
That we need not be forever lost.

Christ's love was made manifest,
He died that wretched death.
In Gethsemane, the battle won;
Prayed, "Not my will, but, Thine be done."

Those who trust Christ need never fear.
Their salvation is secure.
God in His love gave this plan;
For the redemption of fallen man.

We are weak, earthy and frail,
But, our loving God loves us still.
His love abides and never fails.
God's love, so great, never fails.

Heaven

and

Hell

Time is Wasting

(Villanelle)

While time is wasting here below;
Uncaring hearts, the conscience sear,
Sinful man judged by seeds they sow.

Since man has proven his own foe,
God in His mercy, one should fear;
While time is wasting here below.

God's plan is plain … so man can know,
Christ is the Way … His Son so dear;
Sinful man judged by seeds they sow.

Through Christ … Salvation … God bestows,
By grace through faith, God's love is near,
While time is wasting here below.

Redeem the time; His voice says, "Go!"
Some will accept Christ when they hear;
Sinful man judged by seeds they sow.

All without Christ will reap sin's woe;
Torment in Hell when Christ appears;
While time is wasting here below,
Sinful man judged by seeds they sow.

God's River

A New Heaven and a new earth are promised in
    God's Holy Word ...
If all is NEW ... then that which is old – is
    passed away from here on earth;
When the Angel, Michael, blows the trumpet and
    time shall, be no more –
Everything begins – again ... not to be known as
    it was before.

The Pure River of Water of Life proceeds out from
    the Throne of God and of the Lamb.
With the Tree of Life in the midst of the street
    of it, and on either side –;
Nothing of the polluted sea or tributaries ... hence-
    forth (regardless of beauty) anything known to
       man ...
Shall be there, or have the least part in Heaven's
    ecological site.

God made a way ... that all can enjoy this beautiful
    river ... having a part –;
He sent His only begotten Son ... because He loved
    the world ... to die in our stead;
When a person accepts Christ as their Saviour ...
    they're given a new heart ...
Now is the time ... a decision to make ... to delay,
    is with danger to tread.

It's Up To You

There are two roads ... one leads to Heaven and the other
    to Hell ...;
If in your choosing you've chosen the narrow road, you've
    done well –;
The broad road is the most traveled one ... headlong to ...
    destruction running;
For the Bible does say ... "Hell hath enlarged itself to
    meet thee at thy coming."

The narrow road is the one along which Christ ... does always
    lead ...;
Scrutinizing all motives ... judging righteously each and ...
    every deed –;
He keeps watch ... searching our hearts and knows if we
    belong to Him;
If things are there ... which shouldn't be ... God's chastening
    to some is grim.

When accepting Christ as Saviour ... we choose the narrow
    road ...;
It's while living here on earth ... preparation is made as to
    where will be our eternal abode –;
Each will answer God's clarion call ... for we're judgment
    bound ... one and all;
It matters not if ... living when Christ returns or ... in
    death when we hear our name called.

It's Your Choice

You choose your own way …;
Heaven, or Hell's wrath –;
While on earth you live;
Soul lives when life's gone;
Death has naught to say;
While day … choose your path;
Heart to Christ need give;
He'll save … He alone.

Nothing good we've done;
For Heaven to see …
Because of God's love;
We approach His Throne;
Through Jesus, His Son –
Who died to set free;
He's gone on before …
To welcome us home.

After the Grave

For all the living know that they shall die,
But, the dead know not anything at all;
Neither have they anymore a reward;
The memory of them is quite forgotten.

Their love and their hatred and their envy,
Is perished, neither have they any portion;
Forever in anything that is done …
Dead have no part in life under the sun.

The grave is just a place the body rests,
Waiting the resurrection … of saved or lost;
The spirit goes back to God who gave it;
To rest in peace, if saved … torment if lost.

The grave cannot hold the spirit of man.
Only an empty, "shell" inhabits the grave;
After resurrection, in judgment we stand;
A different one for the lost, than the saved.

Eternity's settled, while living on earth,
Only in life, a decision is made …
Through accepting God's Son, comes the New Birth;
Christ shed His life's blood, the sin debt He paid.

The devil

Lucifer, the devil, was in the Garden of Eden.
He was one of the archangels.
The earth was his territory over which to rule.
He came to Eve in the form of a serpent;
Asking her questions – doubts to fuel.
He, being more subtle – to her destruction lent;
She being deceived – ate of the forbidden tree,
Then gave to her husband – as if on a mission sent.

God placed a curse upon the serpent;
Cursed above all cattle and beasts of the field;
"Upon thy belly" – God's curse rang;
"And dust to eat all thy life – Nothing but strife

Between thee, and the woman,
Between thy seed and her seed."
Adam was not deceived – eyes open –
Listened to his wife.

The ground was cursed because of Adam.
In sorrow would he toil, to bring forth food,
Midst thorns and thistles as best he could.
Ever since this – has been the lot of man.
Eve's sorrow was multiplied – and in conception.
She allowed her rebellion to get out of hand.
Her desire to be to her husband because of her defection.
And he shall rule over thee – in the land.

If Adam and Eve would have given heed,
To instructions given them of God,
They could have eaten of the tree of life;
Instead of the tree of good and bad.
They made their choice and disobeyed;
God placed at the east of the Garden of Eden cherubims
With flaming swords turning as – He bade.
To keep man in his sinful state – away from the Tree of Life.

Lucifer was not satisfied with his station given
He said, "I will be like the most High;
I will ascend above the heights of the clouds
    I will ascend into heaven;
I will exalt my throne above the stars of God."
But, God said, "O Lucifer, son of the morning!
How thou art cut down to the ground, which did weaken the
            nations!
For thou has said in thine heart, I will ascend into Heaven,
Yet, thou shalt be brought down to hell, to the sides of the pit."

Comfort, Hope and Inspiration

—

Faith

Faith is the substance of things hoped for,
The evidence of things not seen …
The condition of the mind can overcome many hardships,
That otherwise would devastate a life.
Depression comes when giving up hope.
Looking to ourselves and within ourselves,
Thinking not of others but only of self.
And seeing one's weaknesses brings despair.
Faith is the opposite of doubt;
When we raise our eyes above earth's horizon
Looking to the Lord high above the hills
For strength to do what we should do,
Letting Him lead: for unlike us, He sees all:
He can see around every bend, in life's road,
Knowing all things, He will lead us aright;
In adverse times, we are still to lean.
For if we belong to Him, He'll never
Leave us or forsake us because of our
    trust put in Him as Saviour of our soul,
Accepting Him as our own personal Saviour
    through faith and repentance,
He gives us strength for all in life;
The Apostle Paul said nothing could
Separate us from the love of God, which is in Christ Jesus
    our Lord.
All the devil does to us comes through
    the permissive Will of God,
God is stronger than the devil:
The kind of faith acceptable to God
    overcomes adversity.
Reeds are tossed and shaken with the wind,

While the Oak bends, but doesn't bow.
We trust our soul into the Lord's safekeeping.
Why then do we fail to let Him lead us through life?
If He can keep our soul in safekeeping …
As He says in His Word He will do,
Then as He knows … every sparrow that falls
We should know he watches o'er us,
And will until we leave this life in death;
Then a Home in Heaven awaits all
    those saved …
Adversity in life makes us grow … moving
    closer to the Source of our strength.
As the roots of the giant Oak tree reach ever deeper
    into the soil for nourishment and water.

Faith Delivers

The wicked flee when no man pursueth,
While the righteous are as bold as lions.
As a man thinketh in his heart so is he …
Without faith, it's impossible to please God.

Three Hebrew children in a fiery furnace …
Because of their faith, God delivered them.
Christ was there among the flames … giving grace;
Daniel's faith saved him from the lion's den.

God's Word says, "Buy the truth and sell it not!"
In the time we live … TRUTH is auctioned cheap:
It's Heaven or Hell … man chooses his lot …
Man turning from the truth, trouble does reap.

God made man a little lower then than angels.
God has a plan for redeeming the lost;
It's by grace through faith in Christ, His Word tells:
A gift of God ... not of works ... none can boast!

Faith
(Think and Dream)

You must think ... and you must dream ...
    dreams;
... Without this ... "time out" – from life's usual
    race;
There would be no excellence –if thinking and
    dreams – weren't an integral part – it deems –
And the thinking process ... laced with faith – must
    be the base.
For faith is of the essence – if we would please
    God ... this is His means ...;
To allow man to accomplish things that would
    otherwise, be left untried ... to save face.

So pray – as you dream ... you must –
    if you desire life to be a lofty game.
Enlarge your horizons ... flights the mind
    may take – not only for fantasy's sake;
Of all the inventions ever made ... someone
    had to think and dream – it seems.
Anything done acceptable to Christ ... must be
    done by faith.
Take time to dream, think and pray ... close to
    the Lord always stay.
Think with your heart ... not just your mind –
    faith holding doubts at bay!

No one – has ever accomplished … anything –
    that matters;
Without faith … and thinking thoughts
    higher, than mortal man can reach –
Mind and spirit can soar – while the
    body's confined – though the devil batters;
Nothing is impossible with God's help …
    the Bible does teach.
So pray, when you think and dream … having
    faith – with God's help – doubts do scatter;
Christ taught the Apostles to pray – that their faith be
    increased – we need to do so, the same as they!!

Faith is the Substance

Faith causes one to believe
When discouragement comes by degrees.
You just press on – don't turn back
Knowing you'll see whatever you lack.
Faith is the substance of things hoped for,
The evidence of things not seen.
Faith sees light when all is dark
Visualizes sunshine when there's no spark,
Sees a rainbow in the darkened sky,
Anticipates rain when there's a drought.
Espies the silver lining through the clouds.
Faith always seeing what is not!
Faith sees health in sickness coming about.
Hopeful of prosperity, with nothing to doubt,
Faint-hearted – but, faith makes the heart stout.
Faith makes for peace – moves to rout.
Resting secure – safe in God's care
With Christ's help – trusting, believing we can bear.

Only Believe

All things are possible to him that believeth …
In Christ's name, we need ask, with faith,
    help to receive;
We must trust God to provide what's
    needed in life,
Waiting with faith … though dark threads
    with bright ones, He weaves.

He'll not put more on us than we are
    able to bear:
As the Master Weaver, God knows just
    what we need …
And to obey in adversity … we need dare,
Our love is proven not in words, but
    by our deeds.

Walking by sight … in light of the sun, is not faith:
But, pressing on, in the dark, black
    shadows of night …
Seeing as best we can … in faith's light,
    not by sight;
Letting Christ shine in our life,
    the world's only light.

"I Love Thee, Lord"

(an early poem)

"Many are the reasons, Lord, for my
   love toward thee,
Thou art my truest friend,
   and didst from Heaven descend
      to die on Calvary for me.
I love Thee, Lord, I love Thee.

I know that Thou wilt ever
   be kind and loving unto me.
And Thou wilt guide and protect,
   if I only lean on Thee.
Be ever merciful unto me.
I love Thee, I love Thee."

Who Are We?

Who are we? … certainly not always what we seem
to be, think we are, or others see.
We're not on our own to do as we decide or choose,
then run free –
We're not our own … we're bought with God's
required price;
Belonging to the Lord … unless consecrated … will
not the flesh satisfy, but does the soul suffice.

The Lord chastens all those who through Christ –
belong to him …
Chastening never is pleasant at the time, because
of disobedience … it does stem …
Man is vanity in all his fleshly pomp and splendor …
remains the same;
The Spirit born of God, dwelling in a temple God made
from dust … the only eternal thing.

Only One Good

The Lord said … "There is only one good –
    the Father –;"
Whatever good there is in any – is
    only what's of God …;
So – if you see in a person attributes
    glorifying the Father – and no other;
It's the Spirit of Christ within – for man
    is earthy … he's of the sod –;

With the Lord's help, we can be of
    good influence –;
Leading others to the truth, and them accepting
    Christ as Saviour …
As we have no goodness within ourselves,
    it's the only way that makes for endurance.
If we would bask in God's blessing and
    approval – we must seek His favor.

When our attention is brought to focus
    on a person's deeds or actions …;
If it honors God … we are only what
    we are –
        by God's matchless grace –;
Honor should be to the Lord … there
    should be no faction –
His strength is ours – when we are weak
    within ourselves –
        always faith our weakness does efface.

Mercy

If mercy is what you want;
Then mercy is what you give.
For with whatsoever judgment you meet;
It will be measured to you again.
We can't just say, "Go and be ye filled;"
Also, "Go and be ye warm" – is banned.

We need give to one who's hungry;
As with water their cups we fill.
Bread cast upon the waters;
To you will return again –.
Be considerate of feelings of others;
Their needs as your own – discern.

Doing for Christ means doing for others,
He'll accept it as done unto him.
If we are helpful to the least of the brethren;
We show our love for Christ, – ministering to them.
All these things the Bible teaches;
We just pray the lesson we'll learn!

God's Will or Mine!

"Lord, not my will, but Thine be done;"
I said, finishing my prayer …;
When time comes … my own way or none –
With self-will on a tear.

Oh, no! Not that place … not for me;
Over there who can see?
That other place I'd like to be;
Do hope you will agree.

Location and weather's just right;
The place cut out for me …
I'll be exalted to great height –;
It'll be known … all can see.

Humbly??? … I thought to pray again!
Could I have my own way?
Thoughts kept running … as they began;
Selfishly … through the day.

When listening quietly from the start;
… A whisper … deep inside …
Comes from the depth of my own heart;
Where God's love does abide.

Bringing to mind something I knew …
The clay has naught to say –
Vessel formed … not Potter in lieu;
Not … Potter, … just … the clay.

Lighting the Way

The Bible is a lamp unto our feet …;
As we travel life's treacherous highway,
If we fail to learn – we're blinded … unable to see;
Night without the passing … unable to turn to day.

Do we hold a light for others … warning of the abyss?
Showing others Christ, our Saviour … along life's way;
If we ourselves stumble on in darkness,
How can we to others show … the light's ray?

Light chases the darkness away …;
Lost souls are heard to say, … "Where, oh, where is the light?"
The dark covering of sin will stay;
Until in mercy, light is shown to win through night.

God's Word … a lamp, shows feet where to walk …
But, when lives exalt God's plan –;
The lamp held high, gives forth to souls the light sought;
Reaching many throughout the land.

All know … even a candle when held high …
Gives forth much more light –;
Than when set on the floor … feet hovering just above it.
Just as the candle, God's word highly esteemed in lives shines
         bright.

No use to climb the highest hill …;
Shine a light toward the clouds –,
Lighting not your own path over the rocks, but standing still;
If your own way is illuminated, Christ held high … light reaches
  to the crowds.

Tunnel of Life

Is that a light … at the end of the tunnel …
  shining brightly for me …?
Midst all the dark clouds … a bright light is
  visible … surely I see –;
Whether seeing the light with the spirit … by
  faith or … seeing the light by sight …
It matters not who viewed the end of the tunnel's
  light …
Keep looking up … to God who is All-Powerful and
  in control;
And the one to be feared … who is able to cast
  into Hell both body and soul;
Faith brings light when all around with darkness
  oppressed …
Doubts bring dark tunnels overhung with clouds
  … that distress.

When drawn away from the shelter and protection
  of our Lord – by doubts …
Allowing all light to be obscured at the end of
  the tunnel – going 'round about;
To have life and have it more abundantly – is why
  Christ came on Calvary to die …
Without faith, it's impossible to please God …
  that's where the trouble doth lie.
God is love … He loved us so – His only begotten
  Son … He gave …
That all who would believe in Christ … their soul
  He would save.
When your life becomes a dark tunnel – of troubles
  and despair … faith will prevail;
Take time to repent and pray … for Jesus can never
  fail.

A Nice Surprise

Tell me, who doesn't like a nice surprise?
Of course, it must be a nice one … true;
If it be a good deed – or gift causing a sigh;
Even those who say they don't – being
  not persuaded – I believe they do!

Patience

Patience is something we need to acquire;
If not to some extent … life can be dire …
Many happenings in life – taut the nerves as a band;
Best to batten down … advice to every woman and man.

God's word says, "Tribulation worketh patience;"
Acquiring patience causes one to be more gracious.
We pray for patience … then are astonished when trials come.
God has heard – answered our prayer, to others – more than some.

To serve the Lord in an adult way …;
We shouldn't expect as an irresponsible child to stay;
God needs servants, who with faith do pray,
And not "fall by the wayside" in adversity's day.

Compassion

When someone is in spiritual or physical need;
One needs respond with compassionate speed;
If you wait until all's perfect with you;
They'll go unattended … nothing you'll do.

We're to give or provide whatever with care;
Doing as if unto the Lord … our hearts laid bare.
God doesn't expect that … we have not –;
But, does want willing service, whatever our lot.

Manifold needs come to all to some extent;
When our help is needed … not to resent.
Discouragement is a much worn tool of the devil;
He uses it on all – not a few or several.

While assisting with whatever one's need;
Continue to pray God will bless with all speed;
Yet, be prepared to stay the course …
In God's own time, will it come
    about … not to force.

In God's work, we are plainly taught;
"My grace is sufficient" … no scripture for naught;
To please our Lord, faith and trust are of the essence;
Do not quit or fall by the wayside – run the distance.

In a Crowd

"Speak up! Speak up, I say, my man!
I'm trying to hear you, if I can.
Don't be shy like a maid,
Hiding behind her inadequate fan …!
If the issue at hand –
Doesn't suit – do reprimand!
Take your place – the space do grace;
Not taking offense, but nothing base.
State the facts – though getting the axe;
Other eyes you may open still.
Anyone desiring right – must fight;
Not be taken against their will.
What a difference one man makes;
When he values the things at stake.
Never passive – for passive's sake;
Even though no one else has shown
Courage to speak – speak alone.
Then as a man … you'll go home!"

"Speak Up"

"Speak up I say, while you may,
Fill your place; take your stand.
As long on earth as you delay,
Decision to make of you demands.
Responsible for our actions –
    each day;
Can't escape by traveling the lands.
Keeping quiet such a price to pay;
Better met – draw a line in the sand.
Speak up I say – from time of birth –
You cannot shirk
    what's left to us."

Choices While Decision

While living you have a choice
As to what your decision will be.
You have only yourself to blame.

Let God Fight For You

Fight back … is something inborn in humanity to always
  do …
A child may be bullied by someone … if afraid or someone bigger than they –;
But, eventually they'll get fed up … There's a saying –
  "every dog has his day;"
It's only natural for each person to want to have his
  say –;

A person sometimes … when pushed so long and under
  continual pressure …
Will break in spirit … leaving of what once was …
  merely a token –;
Especially when ill health and adverse living conditions …
  cause heartache beyond measure;
When neglect comes from those who are responsible and
  should have given care … waiting to see spirit broken.

The way to fight back … let the Lord do the fighting …
  and the spirit within will heal and be revived …
When it comes to getting even for ill treatment … let
  God … He can turn things about –;
He sees and knows all – even the sparrow that falls … never
  neglects us when we call, with Him we survive.
"Vengeance is mine," saith the Lord – "I will repay …"
  when He is ready … no detour on route.

Oh, the peace of mind – when all is left … to an All-
  Knowing – All-Seeing God …
Who loves and cares … broken hearts He heals and lovingly
  repairs –;
Only He knows how to lift you, … while He applies the
  chastening rod.
So … fight back with prayer and supplication and peace
  of mind – be of good courage … disdain despair.

Go With What You Know

Do you accuse one you know nothing …
    about;
Better than face up to what you know
    is true …
Better stick with what you know is true,
    without doubt;
Judging one without the facts is nothing
    new.

God sees ALL … in His light … as it really
    is …
God's no respecter of persons … judging
    right;
Won't work … making excuses for those
    you choose;
God's judging is true … no use what's
    right to fight.

Obedience to God … from all is due
    Him …
God's standard never changes … He's
    always right –
The Bible states … "By their fruits ye
    shall know them;"
We aren't judges … yet, fruit inspectors –
    by sight.

"Lord, help us trust You … accept facts in
    our life …
When hurt by someone close … give strength
    to snap back –
Knowing faith and trust in You quiets all
    strife;
You never fail us … but give us the faith we
    lack."

Living Now

So many say, "Everything has gone wrong …;"
Yet … not all that could have gone –;
Even in the heartache that is today;
Happenings so much worse at our door could lay.
When we're prone to complain and say;
All things have gone awry … but nay –;
Not nearly as much as will and could be;
If we live longer … in time, we'll soon see –
Then to be in as good condition as we are now;
We would never complain again … a vow.

Thankfulness is always much in order;
Our great God fills our lives with blessings to the border.
When you're thinking discouraging thoughts;
Count your blessings … not to become overly fraught;
Always look around you – someone in worse condition,
Many sights to assay, causing a heart's rendition.
Look beyond self – to another's needs;
Help assuage their misery – by word and deed.
The only way to serve the Lord is through humanity;
So with thankful – humble heart – at the foot of the cross,
        lay all vanity.

Be Very Strong

What do you do when things go wrong …?
Do you blame whoever happens along?
Is nothing ever really your fault –
If accusation points your way – do you call a halt?

The Bible says, "Quit you like men…"
God desires we grow up … to wrong not bend.
Sins and shortcomings … are common to all;
Confessed to the Lord … He forgives as on His grace we fall.

He'll never leave or forsake, we're told …
Those who are His through Salvation of their soul –;
Faith and obedience … makes one grow strong;
With hearts dedicated to the Lord … as they belong.

Give or Take

We've all heard the old saying – "Give
   or take a few";
There's more to the saying than
   what seems …;
There are some people who are …
   "givers" … them their due –;
More seem to be of the category –
   of, "takers", it deems …

If you're one or the other … and
   there's never a balance …
Just try to be a "giver" and see
   what a difference it makes –;
If you have only practiced "taking"
   do a switch with no dalliance –;
There's a blessing in putting God first,
   then others – self-denial it takes.

One who always gives – needs to learn
   to be a "taker" at times …
Giving those around a chance to be
   blessed by the doing –;
Whatever we do should be for God's
   honor and glory; this in the Bible we find.
Our lives should be a Christian reflection … God's
   will doing and forever pursuing.

Character Counts

(Skeltonic Verse)

Character does matter!
Bad morals do scatter,
Leaves lives in a tatter;
Some crazier than a hatter!
Personality little avails,
Seen only as a veil,
Stripped beyond the pale,
Many end in jail!
Others on verge to sail …
Personality … did fail.
Too late beyond bars,
Leaving many scars,
Have keys, but no cars!
Better off on Mars;
Can't even see stars!
Thoughts of character come late,
Personality is lightweight,
Not here because of fate,
Didn't choose roommate!
Passed through same gate,
Both filled with hate,
Character counted little,
Those preaching Christ, we riddle;
Did nothing but piddle,
Behind bars in the middle,
Cat and the fiddle,
Pot blacker than kettle,
What's good cast aside!
Preaching couldn't abide,
In wrong ones confide,
Together cried …
Yet, God's Way defied!
No use to hide;
Like to start over …
Even in doghouse with Rover
Singing "White Cliffs of Dover."

Not a Village!
But, Parents

Parents are responsible for the rearing of their own …;
Providing the best that's possible – and from evil to defend;
Giving love with discipline – teaching them of God …
warning them of sin.
The Bible puts responsibility where it belongs from
beginning to end.

To raise a, "child" … where time isn't given, but to a nanny
is sent …;
Is so different from raising, "children" where hours are
from daylight 'till dark;
Endurance because of love … not broken … but back in
labor bent …;
The Bible for guidance, faith in God, depending upon Him
while doing our part.

Individual families make up a village, hamlet, town or
metropolis …;
Wherever a family resides, parents are to care for the
children– they're lent;
A blessing from God … whose training should be a must –;
No, "village" or government is to raise children God has
sent.

Animals have much concern for their own – mankind many
responsibilities spurn;
Beasts of the field and fowls provide for their own; food
and shelter hard to find;
Teaching their little ones to know … they must learn as they
grow …;

To make their own way, each day … among their own kind.
When our Constitution was written, "we the people" in
       heart and mind,
A government – of the people, by the people, and for the
       people … right?
Fighting to stand in the light of liberty … not oppression's
       night …
Living for God, caring for our own, "children" … taking a
       chance of leaving it
          to perhaps the, "Village Idiot" isn't very bright.

Steady On

When troubles o'erwhelm you … pressing you
    down …
God's the only help for man … still on His
    Throne … as before troubles began –;

Faith causes one to trust in God … no matter
    what surrounds;
With the eye of faith … seeing what is not –
    while God's All-Seeing-Eye sees across the land.

When dark cloud's dense fog swirl, whirl …
    mightily … pulling down …
Faith looks up and sees … the beautiful
    Heavenly Home – bequeathed;
Sure footing on solid ground – never looking down,
    trusting God … though to earth we're bound –;
Always soaring … rising above adverse circumstances …
    that's faith's bequest.

So many things in this life … cause heartache …
    sickness, disappointment and strife;
Enduring faith … makes life's pathway show bright …
    shining forth with Heaven's light –;
It matters not … we may forget reason … not even
    remember life or the season …
The maniac of the Gadarenes – worshiped Jesus …
    his healing – delivered from sin's mental dark
       night.

Delight in the Lord

Delight … delight in the Lord should …
    always be …
And not according to our circumstance,
    be enhanced.
Man is of few days and full of trouble,
    of trouble never free –
Delighting ourselves in the Lord … isn't
    to be left to chance.

Delight thyself … in the WAYS – of the
    Lord,
And He WILL give thee … the desires of
    thine heart …
Is promised in the 37th Psalm of His …
    Word –
Delight in the Lord … can only come from
    right; circumstances play no part.

To delight oneself in God's ways, a heart
must be right ...
The thoughts and actions in life will be
of a different sort.
Since we know God's promises are true ...
outlook should be bright.
Trust and faith ... assurance and a safe
haven, on the high seas or in port.

Good rest can be had in a somewhat ...
uncomfortable bed ...
Not leaving to outward conditions, our
delight in the Lord;
But, in faith resting in security, with
peace, in what God's Word says.
A life of faith in service for the Lord ...
at the end of time, has its own rewards.

Somber Thoughts

Midst the heartache and sorrow
In life, that's common to all;
Minds blot out what the heart knows;
When somber thoughts … sins recall.

Life viewed from the mountaintop,
More lighthearted thoughts in charge;
Where man's spirit soars nonstop,
And sin doesn't loom as large.

Somber thoughts search the Spirit …
Seeking welfare of the soul;
Life's valleys have their purpose,
Enriches life manifold.

Reeds are shaken with the wind,
While the giant oak's reach down;
The oak, wind tossed, only bends;
After the storm … reeds not found.

A help to all who know Him,
Our Lord has promised to be;
Works won't be burned as stubble,
When life, with God's Word, agrees.

Somber thoughts bring repentance,
God's Spirit does search the soul;
Condemning what lies between;
And not shining like pure gold.

Low in spirit … just repent;
Exaltation, yours to know …
Only then forgiveness sent;
For God's love can heal all woe.

Sadness

Sadness remains a part of life …
Because of sin, there's sadness;
God's power can be known midst strife,
And with His care, we'll be blest.

Not good works … but faith He asks:
Tells us not to be afraid …
While we in His love do bask;
Earthly troubles seem to fade.

Obedience, our Lord desires …;
And with repentance, tops His list;
If to His grace we aspire,
And the devil we'd resist.

All men are born to trouble
But, in Christ, there's help we find.
Lives can be lived to the full
When love with faith we combine.

Even in sadness, there is joy,
When life centers around Christ,
Each man, woman, girl, or boy
Can claim Him their sacrifice.

So Much Trouble!

It seems life for me is full of trouble!
Right! God's Word plainly states that this is so …
Man born of woman is few days … with trouble;
If you've read the scriptures … you ought to know.

Trouble is a part of life … the lot of man –;
No need to be surprised … or complain,
We're made of the dust, but God has His plan.
Obedience will bring blessings,
      yet again.

Looking Up Only in Affliction!
(Psalm 119:69 & 71)

"Before I was afflicted, I went astray:
But, now have kept thy word," the psalmist said;
And also … "It is good for me that I have
Been afflicted, that I might learn thy statues."

Our trials are not designed to tear us down …
God tries the Christian to purify their faith,
He tests His children to build strong character … sound,
Desiring they choose the path narrow and straight.

If only in affliction we seek the Lord,
When seeking His help … only then looking up …
Knowing God's goodness – thus, trusting He will afford
Mercy through repentance, as with Him they sup.

Misunderstood

Misunderstood … is a universal –
   complaint –;
"No one understands" … the phrase
   begins to sound trite and lank …
Much time the reason for so much
   confusion …
Not taking the time to explain …
   actions – thoughts refusing.

Next time … before … complaining so
   much …
Contemplate awhile – before becoming
   upset with such –
Could be your own fault … you didn't
   take time …;
To explain to one you, often condemn
   for not understanding yet again.

Instead of being misunderstood … as one
   always claims …
Perhaps it's more one's own fault … because
   never really explained –.
Need take responsibility instead of continuing
   to whine …
That "no one understands"… yet, to take time
   to explain … there' s just never time.

Along Life's Way

Along life's way, some days seem lonely and sad,
Mind darting here, there and here stopping; to contemplate.
Such ordeals you have come through – ever so bad;
You still remember vividly, though not the date.
You think if you hadn't done this or maybe if you had,
Perhaps, it could all the differences have made.
Ah, quiet – just be calm, not frantic as someone mad;
Doing your best, without knowing, takes faith in God, not
       fate.
Reliance on Christ is a way of life – not a fad;
That's living by faith as you travel along life's way.

Along life's way – a furrow we plow,
It may be deep or extremely shallow;
Straight as an arrow or crooked; it's up to us, how.
The ground we travel to us is fallow,
So, in reverence to Christ, our Saviour, we bow;
Lest on new ground, with hardships, we become calloused.
Our hearts will harden left untended if we allow.
Then, we will be hopeless, as a candle without tallow!
Experiences in life should cause us to mellow,
Across life's way, sacred ground should become hallowed.

Along life's way we must lean on our Saviour and rest.
Traveling, unsettled, as a wanderer if on our own;
But, when we are exhausted and worn, God's at His best.
While we are struggling, beaten and weary of bone,
Convinced we have made a most terrible mess;
If we but lift our eyes heavenward, up toward home,
We can know security – as a bird in its nest.
With God's loving Arms around us – not alone;

Progressing speedily along toward our heavenly home, no less,
As we travel along life's way, all troubles will soon be gone.

As we travel life's way, struggling as we stumble along;
'Tis as though our eyes are blinded, and we don't see,
Secure in the knowledge that whatever seems so wrong;
Will ultimately in the Judgment, without fail, corrected be;
Then we can join in that long delayed song.
Singing and praising our Lord for setting us free;
Such trials, sickness and hardships a part of us for so long,
Soon disappear – just keep faith and trust, that is the key.
Doubts, fears, anxieties, and tears soon are gone;
Along life's way as we love, pray and persevere, strength is
given to you and me.

Light in the Dark

Such trouble and heartache with
    care –;
If it weren't for the Lord – would be utter
    despair …
Heavy clouds o'ershadow … obscuring the
    silver lining;
Yet, faith sees light shining through – the
    dark with silver combining.

The heart is so bruised – from things passed
    by –;
Yet, strength … God gives – through the tears
    and sighs …
Darkness now – but, the sun is just below the
    horizon;
Faith and trust in the Lord – sees the light
    before it appears – doubts and darkness
       subsiding.

Sunshine does come – though at first flickering –
    clouds drifting slowly another way …
Each life has some heartache – brighter days come …
    not always to stay.
Clouds are an integral part of the tunnel of life –
    also have their part in the tapestry of day –;
Sunshine's golden threads are woven dark and
    silver – faith brightening the way.

In times of heartache and trouble … which every
    life does see –;
Looking beyond self and pity – a flickering beacon
    there'll always be …
Growing stronger as faith – floods the path of life –
    willing always for God to lead;
Trusting and with thankful heart … God will always
    supply our need!

Don't Wait Too Late

The
Wolf is
At the door!
I've tried to push
Him away but seems
He slips around the post;
In many shapes he enters,
Whether the door is open or
He must scrunch up to come underneath:
Be diligent and wise; don't wait on fate!

So Thankful He Cares

Trusting a loved one who's far away;
Into a great God's loving care . . .
Who knows everything . . . night and day;
Our very thoughts to Him laid bare.

Our heart can be at peace in this;
After supplication made by prayer:
Faith needs press forward . . . doubts resist,
By the devil inspired . . . not rare.

We must pray with faith, believing;
That God does hear and answer prayer:
Only through faith, all else leaving;
God can overrule what others dare.

God limits the devil in his power;
He only has what God allows . . .
God is the One man answers to;
The One to whom ALL knees will bow.

If God be for us . . . we can't fail;
In faith and trust with Him proceed,
He's in charge . . . to every detail;
Evil is subject to God . . . decreed.

God can halt evil at His Will;
He has the whole world in His Hands;
Can quiet the storms with "Peace be still;"
His power reaches faraway lands.

Friends

(John 15:13,14 Proverbs 17:17, 18:24 & 22:1)

Jesus said, "Ye are my friends if ye do whatsoever
    I command you."
A man that hath friends must show himself friendly ...
    A good name is better than riches;
As a man thinketh in his heart, so is he;
    And from the heart, words do issue.
Obedience to the Lord's command will keep
    one from the devil's glitches.

One of the greatest blessings of life is true friendship ...
    not the "fair weather kind"!
A true friend will not turn you out in the cold.
There is no friend like the Lord Jesus Christ.
Friendship has no price ... cannot be bought,
    traded, or to highest bidder sold.

True friendship does not run its course ... when
    there's nothing more you can do for "me"!
"Fair weather friends" always consider how certain
    "friendships" will profit them ...
The Lord looks on the heart, nothing escapes Him ...
    every motive He does see ...
True repentance is needed ... for all duplicity, from
    the heart does stem.

"Greater love hath no man than this, that a
    man lay down his life for his friends:
Christ died on Calvary for our sins: while we
    were yet sinners, he loved us …
Jesus said, "Ye are my friends, if ye do whatsoever
    I command you."
Abraham was known as a friend of God; his
    faith was counted as righteousness.

… "There is a friend that sticketh
Closer than a brother …" Jonathan and David's
    friendship intertwined with love …
"A friend loveth at all times, and a brother
    is born for adversity."
"Choose a good name rather than great riches …
    loving favor rather than silver and gold!"

Someone Besides

In a room full of people …
Do you try others to make feel at ease?
A friendly smile will change what's dull;
Not waiting … for each their inclinations to appease.

Concerning oneself with feelings of others …;
Takes a certain humility and understanding;
If each stood back waiting for another –;
Communication would be … nothing demanding.

Others may feel the same as you …
But, waiting for someone to take the lead;
To have friends …friendliness you must pursue.
Showing empathy, manifest itself in every deed.

Our remembrance should be … we're not alone;
Many in shadows drift … needing a lift.
Standing back as gone lack … man is prone.
With consideration for those around and tactics shift.

Forgetting self … not standing apart …
Drawing those out, so sedate … shyness to abate;
Thinking of others, to lose one's self is the place to start;
Bound up in self can be overcome; it's selfishness not fate.

"Lord, Help Me"

"Lord, I pray Thee, help me,
To tell what's in my heart;
To those around 'bout me,
Who are walking in the dark.

Lord, may I not falter, ever,
To witness as I can;
To those who need Thy comfort;
May I lend a helping hand.

Lord, I would draw closer to Thee,
To have the strength I need;
To help some poor lost sinner,
And in the right way lead.

Lord, help my faith grow stronger,
In spite of all adversity;
That I might help a child of Thine,
To heavily on Thee lean.

Lord, help me know my weakness,
The stronger in body I seem;
That you may receive all glory,
For all things good are from Thee.

Lord, help me to always be thankful,
For loved ones, dear friends, and all;
Who in the time most needed,
Were there without even a call.

Lord, help me to always be thankful,
For prayers and all kindnesses shown;
For every token of love for me,
And for my Dear Loved Ones at home.

For all these things I thank Thee."

"Dear Lord, Help Us All"

"Dear Lord ... I ask Your help, not only me, but
    all ...;
For surely every one who should ... must already
    know –;
That each will answer ... when their name, You
    call;
As well Your own child ... as the Godless
    foe:

Man would exalt himself to heights that only
    to You are known;
His mind filled with vanity ... he continues to
    pursue ...;
If possible, some would fain sit upon Your own
    Throne –;
Desiring to be as God ... as the devil declared
    he would do.

Please help us realize we must have forgiveness
    to improve ...;
Believing all who come to You in repentance ...
    You'll not cast out –;
We should feel ourselves a debtor ... from no man
    removed;

Christ died in our stead … trusting Him will cast
   out doubt."
We're taught not to think of ourselves more highly
   than we ought;
The only good in man is the Spirit of God … when
   he's born again.
Had man been perfect … our Salvation wouldn't
   have had to be bought.
Only in obedience and allegiance to Christ does
   God receive glory from man.

Calm Midst the Storm

Why get excited if things in life's plan
   work out differently? … They surely can –;
Just calm down … look all around –
   it could all be – perhaps will be, much worse …
Nothing can be guaranteed – ever in this
   life, to remain the same;
Troubles are a part – getting their start –
   in Eden with the fall of man – bringing the curse.

Accepting Christ as Saviour with faith
   leaving the directing of one's life to Him –;
Makes a smooth, "plateau" to rest from the
   storm troubles … that careen …
At times – if taken unawares, in the turmoil
   and confusion – pushing … all but over the rim;
But, settled in place – midst God's grace …
   no matter the race – faith shielding from
     stormy winds … though buffeted – life
      can still be serene.

Real Comfort

Best adhere to the things you know …
Don't be led astray because, of some saying so –;
Never change your beliefs just to seem smart;
Or in something untrue, you'll likely take part.

Whatever the Bible states will come to pass …
At the end of time … many will be aghast –;
God's Word is always the basis;
In obeying it … our life can be an oasis.

Put no confidence in the flesh …
But, when trusting the Lord … heart and spirit will mesh;
Christ, the Saviour, is the rock of our Salvation –
All man-made plans we're to shun – no benefit to anyone.

Rejecting Christ as Saviour … leaves only Hell …
Those refusing … in the judgment all will not be well;
The power of choice God gives to man –
Matters not where one may dwell throughout the land.

According to the Scriptures, time for man is running out;
If you don't believe it … study will do away with doubt.
God gave His only begotten Son, the sacrifice for sin …
Christ stood as a Lamb slain … before time did begin.

Thankfulness to God for His wonderful gift …
Should always be remembered … giving hearts a lift.
In the midst of troubles, peace will forever stay –
For our Lord is always there … pointing the way.

Such comfort … real comfort, in knowing Christ as Saviour;
Trusting and believing in God's Son … nothing good we've
      done;
The Bible tells us … He always cares for His own …
There's security for the believer in knowing if we're His;
      Heaven's our home.

At Peace

At peace … though living midst a
      spirit's war –;
A calming effect … faith does bring about …
Talking to our Lord in prayer … the
      best remedy by far –
Trusting the Lord to see us through –
      is faith without doubt.
Surrounded by hostilities and adversities
      on every side …
Yet, leaving to trust the Lord … Who delivers …
      He never leaves you alone –;
In His love and jurisdiction in
      confidence to abide;
A present help in time of trouble … yet, nothing
      wrong does He condone.

Basking in the sunshine of His wonderful,
      matchless love …
Brings a soothing of the spirit to a heart – attuned to God –;
The gift of salvation is by grace to those who desire it …
      a gift from above.
Our Lord reaching down from Heaven, mindful of His child …
      though lowly … akin to the sod.

There's A Reason

Perhaps the situation you find yourself in,
Gives you an opportunity to show what's right;
By faith prove true … and do, as God would have all men,
Not cower as a coward, but with His Word, shine the light.

Sometimes life's outlook at best is dreary and cold,
Not understanding the "why" of things being so;
But, trusting the Lord gives strength and keeps the mind whole,
Discouragement … the devil's best tool, and man's worst foe.

There must be a purpose on you being where you are;
With eyes focused on Heaven, see what life affords …
Serving the Lord by faith is the best life by far,
For without faith, it's impossible to please God.

There are some who always try to help you along;
Your adversity brings opportunity to them …
Living faith in the Lord can't help but make one strong;
The devil brings doubt and with doubt … faith will grow
dim.Though heavy low-hanging shadows threaten o'erhead,
If heart is set on the Lord, and He is your guide,
There can be peace in a life when by the Spirit led;
The Lord cares for His own, and with them will abide.

Astonished was I that those presumed to be friends,
In adversity just turned their head, and winked their eyes;
Help God sent from far and near more than made amends …
Trust not in the flesh, but in God who is all wise.

The Past

The past has slipped away …
Except, of course … the things that stay;
No calling back to undo or do –;
That's a warning to me, and each of you.

Whatever is done in part remains –;
No matter if enlightened and actions disdain.
Time is gone never to return …;
But, not all wasted … if by it we learn.

Perhaps in reflecting on what has gone before;
Will be the best teacher … though heart is sore –;
The Lord in our life can help redeem the time;
Correcting mistakes, "NOW" … easier to find.

The past cannot hinder the decision you make.
Whether you will spend eternity in Heaven or Hell's fiery
    lake.
Christ's blood covers our sin – past sins are forgiven when
    you receive the Lord.
Your destination is settled – Heaven a gift, not a reward.

Reviewing the past can have its effect …;
Seeing the failings of a life that's a wreck –;
Accepting Christ as Saviour is needful for all,
For each one will answer "God's roll of death call."

Reflecting on the past can be beneficial when viewed;
Or can cause discouragement, to be eschewed.
Accepting Christ as Saviour changes a life,
Though commitment to right … doesn't eliminate strife.

Can't Change the Past

A person can never change what's the past!
How the past is viewed ... can change the future;
For when one looks back, the lessons are VAST,
So many deep hurts, could use a suture.

The Lord would have us, continue to learn,
From our experiences ... whether, good or bad;
When desiring right ... evil we discern ...
A life filled, only with regrets ... is sad.

All the, "past" is, as if in cement ... cast –!
For the rest of, "life" there are choices at stake;
Soon future's "now" ... "now's" the past – none does last;
Knowledge from past ... should help choices to make.

God can make, of one's past life ... a clean slate;
In forgiveness, only ... is the, "past" changed,
Christ is the way ... the door ... to Heaven's gate;
Past can be forgiven ... not rearranged!!!

"Now" – Between the Past and Future

The past is gone …
The future not yet born … perhaps for you, never to arrive.
"NOW" … a swiftly fleeting moment … nothing to reject or
    loan;
Wedged between the past and future – only, "NOW" you are
    alive.

To make the most of, "NOW" is of the essence …;
It will be called the past before so very long.
When, "NOW" has slipped from the present –;
It does forever … leave a residue for right … or wrong.

Behold "NOW" is the accepted time – "NOW" is the day of
    Salvation.
God gave His Son to die on Calvary, … to save our sin-sick
    soul.
Christ died for all people … in every nation;
Salvation is a gift … free to all … in God's Word we're told.

The Future

The future looms around the corner of Now …;
Out of sight … not knowing if it will come or how –;
But, looking to the future with faith in the Lord;
Gives strength and comfort … being faith's reward.

Trusting the Lord … not looking back;
The future can be faced … nothing to lack –;
Never to base the future on happenings of the past;
For in God's Hands, circumstances can change fast.

Reflecting on the past can be beneficial when viewed;
Or can cause discouragement to be eschewed …;
Accepting Christ as Saviour changes a life –;
Though commitment to right … doesn't eliminate strife.

Time Doesn't Change Everything

If what you do and what you say –;
Are as far apart as night and day …
When we say … what we'll do –;
To do what we say … not something in lieu;
Not just talking with enthusiasm …
But, to accomplish what's talked, one should pursue;
Everyone … not just a minority of a few …
Detest a prevaricator, with commitments he eschews.

"A man is as good as his word" …
In olden times was prevalent statement heard;
The, "axiom" which so many hearts stirred,
Was a cloak for many … being staunchly gird –;
Values remain the same … whatever the age;
They never take wing and fly as the bird …
Long ago a man was only as good as his word;
Thinking to change what's proved true through the annals
    of time, would be absurd!

Even in Changed Circumstances

Everything is different … all is changed …;
Life is still ever toward eternity moving –;
Time has in life many things rearranged;
Yet, in turmoil and strife, God's presence is soothing.

Whatever obstacles … God's grace is sufficiently supplied;
Trust and faith reach to the great power in Heaven …
God, who controls all things, can a broken heart and spirit
revive;
Every good and perfect gift comes from God – without sin's
leaven.

Changes in life many times leave a thread of fear …
Until there's abiding faith … not seeing the ending is
heartrending;
Where there's faith … a God Who knows ALL, is forever near.
When placing our trust in Him … one knows power from
Heaven's descending.

Stopping to think and pray makes things easier to understand.
As to why such happenings have all come about –;
For those who love the Lord … all things work together for
good;
Faith in the Lord, mattering not changes in route, ever trust, not
doubt.

Ode on Happiness

(Romans 14:22)

Happy is he that does not condemn …
Himself in that thing which he alloweth;
Constraining fleshly nature so grim,
To God boweth.

Satisfied with his own lot in life,
If it be exalted or abased …
Thereby escaping much of the world's strife,
Through Christ by faith.

Truly seeking God's Will, not his own,
Cast all troubles into greater hands;
Natural man to wrong choices are prone;
God will set bands.

A sincere desire God's Will be done,
Always smoothes much of life's confusion;
Trust and faith, the ways to overcome …
Sight's victory won.

Contentment with peace is happiness,
It's far above rubies … without price;
Each life Christ can abundantly bless,
Because of God's sacrifice.

True Happiness

You want to be happy, too, of course, you do …
To be happy … can't be bought – neither by riches or fame–;
Happiness abides in heart and mind – together combined;
Being happy isn't living trouble-free … life only a game.

The Bible plainly states, … "Happy is the man …
Who doesn't condemn himself … in that which he allows:"
Staying close to the Lord … doing right as best we can;
Trusting the Lord to lead … while in prayer we bow.

A person with a clear conscience – God's Word the base;
Is happy not condemning himself in deed's he's done.
Salvation is by grace through faith … has always been God's
        plan.
Obedience is for rewards, not salvation … in life's
    race we run.

Keep Looking Up!

Keep looking up … from Heaven comes our strength.
… Christ died that we might live …!
Not leaving us guessing … just giving a hint;
The very reason God's Son was sent …!
Salvation is simple – believe in Christ and repent.
God gave us His best though His heart was rent!

Keep looking up … eyes toward Heaven;
Many irritating things you'll fail to see.
An increase in faith … praying it is given;
Helps over the hurdles and obstacles that be.
As long as on earth we continue living;
We're never from the effects of sin set free!

Keep looking up … don't despair …!
With eyes of faith, victory's assured –.
Our Heavenly Home is awaiting us there.
After trials and troubles we've endured;
Then to the mansion – Christ has gone to prepare.
All are weak, compared to God – He is the One to fear!

Seasonal

and

Occasional

Thank God for the Pilgrims

(Triolet)

In the year of sixteen hundred and twenty,
By God's grace, the Pilgrims came to Plymouth Rock;
With faith in God, they sailed on the Mayflower
In the year of … sixteen hundred and twenty,
Trusting God's Providential care and power;
Desiring religious freedom not be mocked;
In the year of … sixteen hundred and twenty,
By God's Grace, the Pilgrims came to Plymouth Rock.

Christmas Tree

Christmas tree? There's no such tree by
    name …
Yet, many trees are so called and varied
    besides –;
The cedar, evergreen, spruce, and pine are
    "Christmas tree" – names of fame –;
Many others are decorated – imagination
    being the guide.

A large branch of a tree … bare and painted
    white …
Decorated with Christmas ornaments, icicles
    and such –;
Having seen even a tumbleweed – strung
    with all color lights …
Different from the traditional Christmas tree …
    very much.

Christmas trees are fun for many – old
    or young … just any –;
The tree has nothing to do with the real
    meaning of Christmas –.
The baby Jesus – God's only begotten Son –
    born in a manger – sent to die for men;
All who believe in Jesus – accepting Him
    as the Christ … can be saved with the rest.

The real meaning of Christmas should
    never be forgotten …
It should ever be read and reread to
    one and all –;
Renewing the truths in hearts and minds,
    given in the Scriptures of God's only begotten …
The ransom of the human race from the
    devil – because man in the Garden of Eden did fall.

Enjoy the love of family and friends at …
    Christmastime with presents around your tree –;
But, remembering it was the birth of Christ
    that we celebrate this time of year …
All the enjoyment that comes about …
    or that will ever be …
Should never cause hearts to forget the
    true meaning of Christmas – continuing
        to hold Christ ever dear.

The Heart Can Still Know, Though the Tinsel Goes

Each year Christmas comes
   … Christmas goes,
Still remembered is
   "Sharon's Rose";
Christ came to earth so long
   ago …
God's promised Saviour we
   all know.

After the tree is taken down,
And gifts are left in diminished
   mound;
There's peace that comes
   from knowing Christ;
For Salvation He paid God's
   price.

The merchandising of
   Christmas …
An excuse for some to get
   gain;
The true meaning of it will
   bring
Joy to the heart … while
   angels sing.

While you wait for one day
   each year
There's 364 that's dear …
Christ will never leave or forsake,
When He as Saviour you do
   take.

Bells of Christmas

Bells ringing Christmas morning,
Ringing out across the riven snow –;
Sounding bright and cheery …
Clearly they sound to the hills and valleys low –;
Spirits uplifting … nothing dreary –;
As worshippers to God's House do go …
Though air is cold – hearts are warm and merry …
Silver bells … they're certainly not – but sound
    silvery so!

Love

Love … but love has many dimensions
Love for one another – our love for our Saviour
God's love for us – His love for the whole world –
To love means to give – we can give
Without loving, but never can we love without
Giving. "God so loved the world He gave
His Only Begotten Son – that whosoever
Believeth in Him, should not perish, but
Have everlasting life." God's was the best He
Had – the Jewel of Heaven. Our best is
Due Him as we journey through life.
Whether it's Christmas season or any
Other season, we need always be true –
Yet, seek for peace and not strife.

Whose Birthday?

(Cinquain)

Christmas …
The birth of Christ:
Tinsel, tree, bells ringing
Gifts received by everyone … but
Jesus

Now's the Time

Oh, now's the time … with mistletoe
   hung on every rafter –;
To steal a few kisses … and a time
   to remember ever after.
Before the girls are made aware – if
   it's possible to stick a piece in their hair …
Kisses will be ever coming to me … all
   those other boys … surely won't dare.

Retreat Or Advance

If you need the mistletoe before there's
    any romance …;
The life you live together … needs more
    than mistletoe to enhance –;
Caught under the mistletoe … you just
    could be kissed by the wrong one – not by chance.
Then you'll have to … quickly … like … retreat,
    instead of advance.

The Newborn King

The birth of Christ … we call, "The Christmas
  Story" –;
Christ was born in a manger – no room
  for them in the inn …
God, looking down from Heaven – in all
  His righteous glory –;
Protecting the baby and guiding both Joseph –
  and the baby's mother, Mary …
At Jesus' birth … the shepherds in the fields watching their
  flock;
Saw the glory of the Lord that shown 'round
  about them – angels telling of Christ's birth –;
As the shepherds carefully watched over
  their flock that night …
God, in His Wisdom, watched over all – as
  His only begotten Son was born on earth.
God sent His only begotten Son to earth
  to die for men …
Not as a king in great glory did He come –
  as could have been …
But, as a Babe … tiny and helpless – but with
  Mary and Joseph to love and defend …
God is over all – no one stronger – He is where
  wisdom begins –.
All-Powerful, All-Knowing, All-Seeing …
  on Him, all life depends –;
God was His Father … Mary, His mother –
  from an earthly father He did not descend.
What a wonderful gift God gave when,
  from Heaven … Christ – He did send …
To die for the world – God gave His only
  Begotten Son – everlasting life, to all who
    would believe – one by one – hearts to win.

What Gifts for Christ?

Christmas, to me, is winter's favorite time …
    Christmas is almost here …;
At Christ's birth, the Three Wise Men went to find –
    Jesus, the Babe … with hearts full of cheer –;
Desiring to see the Saviour … to Bethlehem they
    did go; traveling far … gifts they brought there.
Their love to the Saviour, they did show … faith in
    God, leading by a star, turned away fear.

A desire for the Truth is pleasing to God we find …
    after accepting Christ for the Salvation of our soul;
In repentance and faith, giving Him our heart for all
    time; come boldly to God's throne, we're told.
Do we bring gifts to the One who loved us so … on His
    birthday … do we forget – leaving Him out?
Shopping … giving gifts to others wherever we go …
    our hearts are what the Lord wants – no doubt.

God looks on the inside, not as others see … a broken
    spirit and a contrite heart, He does require;
Without faith, it's impossible to please Him … and to
    please Him, we should desire …
Much we can do to show our love to the One who sent His
    Only begotten Son to die for our sin …
Sent the One so near his heart … He came to us from
      above;
To please the Lord, with yielded life and heart …
    each day repent … no one is infallible … repent.

Lest We Forget

Midst all the hustle and bustle …
Christmas cards … to be sent –;
Listening you'll hear gifts a rustle;
All on deadline … are bent.

Much to do … always at the last;
Many things left undone …
Always the same – as in years' past;
But, isn't Christmas fun?

Enjoy Christmas celebration …
But, don't forget what's true;
Your Salvation on Christ's birth hung;
… He was crucified for you.

From the foundation of the world,
Christ stood as a Lamb slain -;
When Adam sinned, the world was hurled;
Into sin … nothing gained.

Most important … IS … Jesus came;
As a Babe … He came to earth;
Since that time … nothing's been the same,
His Birth … brought the New Birth.

On Calvary, He gave His life's blood,
To save a world from sin …
All could accept Him if they WOULD:
He died, lost souls to win.

Family and friends come together;
Because of God's great love …
To celebrate God's Gift … to earth;
Heaven's Jewel … from above.

An Old Remedy

First day to shop … after Christmas
Stores so busy … lines long;
Shopping with returning … makes a fuss;
While anxious to get home.

Years … it's been used from time to time;
Gifts you buy with … no size …
Colors combine … together fine –
Blessing in disguise … TIES!

No excuse to take a tie BACK:
Not because of color …
With gifts given … must use some tack;
Not change bright for duller.

For men … all that for next year's solved;
But, women wear ties, too, we see …
Easier shopping … it's now resolved;
More TIES for you and me!!!

Another Year???

Another year it'll be for some,
For some, another day won't come;
Time allotted is in God's hands …
Either long life or one that is just begun.

New Year's resolutions pile up,
Unused … to overflow life's cup;
Seldom used and forgotten ones,
Make a long, long list … the total sum.

Inside the heart's the place to start,
Where seat of man's affection is …
Only Christ can make the heart new;
And evil ways desired eschew.

God's Word, the basis for what's right,
Jesus came to give the world light;
God gave His Son … Saviour of man,
To redeem man's soul … only He can.

Salvation isn't … by the year …
It's ETERNAL and grows more dear;
Resolutions … you think to make,
Without the, "HEART" … will a wrong turn take.

It's a decision to accept Christ,
Not resolutions that change a heart:
Another Year ??? No one can tell!
When time's up … it's Heaven or Hell.

Spent, But Not Gone

This year is past, but never gone;
All things on file … not one alone –;
For good or bad … what's done is done;
A lesson is learned – when time is none …
As the new year pushes the old one out;
Providing opportunities … unfolding on route.

In thanking the Lord – and doing His bidding;
Next year, our life of self-centeredness ridding;
Soon another year of pages on which to write;
How will the pages read – in an All-Seeing God's sight?

Looking back with regrets over the year that's spent;
An opportunity to remedy mistakes … to some is lent.
A year, though spent, is still on file …
At the judgment – all will answer – being on trial.

The new year just – coming into view …
Should be a challenge – to everyone – not a few;
To see if, with God's help – an improvement to make …
Correcting things passed – that were a mistake –;

For life should be abundantly lived;
Lived for God … He, when asked, will "always forgive."

Valentine Mine

Dear heart, it's Valentine's Day, 1995.
Looking through these cards, old memories revive.
A very special one I see has tattered lace,
Colors are faded – really effaced!
And the verse inside is completely faded,
But, those words I still remember – stated;

> "I love, love, love you;
> Ever so well – more than
> I can say – or ever tell.
> Next in rhyme – wedding time."

Wedding bells did ring, that's true,
Bells ringing for me and you;
Valentine's Day is remembered still.
With each Valentine, there's still a thrill,
But, none as much or ever 'twill be;
As the scraps of one I hug to me.

For Carl

Today and Always

Today is, "Valentine's Day" – the day of, "Romance" –;
For "Romance" … many take a chance …
Thinking with hearts … instead of head;
Many things occur … wrongly led …
Romance alone isn't a quality that wears;
Mundane, "threads" woven in – all must bear –
All doesn't glitter … so – doesn't glow;
Yet, "true love" ... doesn't tarnish – but grow.

Valentine's Day – one day of the year …
So sad – if love waits for, "one day" … there's fear;
What about the other three hundred sixty-four?
Someone other – more likely will adore …
You wait too long to make a declaration –;
Love with wings and "Cupid's arrow" – fly another direction;
"A bird in hand is worth two in a bush" …
When stuck, "dead center" … best give yourself a push.

Romance should be mixed with reality …
The Valentine for real – deals with legality.
Choose wisely – with God's blessing to bind;
Two hearts entwined – yet, each defined …
Going forward in life … hand in hand –;
Marching in step … yet, a different band …
Each as an individual – hearts closely knit;
In thoughts and deeds … with Valentine wit.

Valentine, It Matters Not
(Triolet)

It's a dream to remember,
Or just a remembered dream;
In May or December …
It's a dream to remember,
Youth remains but a glimmer;
Eyes still sparkle and gleam.
It's a dream to remember,
Or just a remembered dream.

For Carl, with love

The Meaning of Easter
"Come Ye"

God's great invitation has gone out ... continues to
    draw, ... without doubt –;
All who are weary ... there's a place of rest ... the
    Lord says, "Come unto Me."
Why hesitate? ... He tells us not to wait – come to Christ,
    the life-giving Fount.
The invitation is – salvation offered – to all ... to everyone ...
    it's free.
Christ died on Calvary ... shedding His own precious –
    blood ...
That we might live ... forever ... His life He did freely
    give.
God gave the, "Jewel" of Heaven ... our Saviour, His Only
    Begotten Son.
All who believe – repenting of their sins ... accepting
    Him as Saviour – He does forgive.

Christ was crucified – buried, and after three days, arose
    from the grave;
He's already with the Father ... sitting at his right hand;
    a mansion awaits us there ...
All who have accepted Him as their own personal Saviour ...
    are eternally saved –;
The great invitation, "Come Ye" ... to accept CHIRST as
    Saviour ... continues to reach out ... everywhere.

The Meaning of Easter

(Triolet)

God so loved the world, He gave His only Son,
Christ died on Calvary's Cross to save the lost!
When Christ was resurrected, God's plan was done.
God so loved the world, He gave His only Son!!
Over death, hell and the grave, our Saviour won.
Paid for man's redemption at an awful cost.
God so loved the world, He gave His only Son;
Christ died on Calvary's Cross to save the lost.

The Fourth of July

(Triolet)

Independence Day … comes again.
An important day to everyone;
Some to work … to others, work is banned;
Independence Day … comes again,
Celebrations differ across the land,
Fireworks prevalent … add to the fun;
Independence Day … comes again;
An important day to everyone.

Father's Day

Many children in growing up want to be like, "Daddy";
They see him as one to imitate … since just a lass or laddie.
So many things they depend upon him to see about and do –;
Play games, take to school, buy candy and, "pop" are only a few.

Father's day is very important … a message sent;
Not second to Mother's day … as with so many prevalent –;
God's word teaches the father is the head of the household;
And will answer to Him if not leading as told.

Except to provide and pay the bills, many times father is left out;
While the rest of the family together seek another route;
Fathers need exert their God-given privilege and right –;
To lead their families in God's own light.

To be a "father" is an important and serious matter;
Leading one's family right from the start is best … not latter.
Then in Heaven, because of Christ, all can be together;
A father's influence and values … should for the better.

This life is temporal … only a short span;
Father's need influence their families … for the best they can;
Training and nurturing in things of the Lord –;
For eternity will tell if right was ignored.

The Judgment Seat of Christ and God's Great White Throne;
Each person will stand at one … before gaining his final home.
God's Judgment is for the lost … Hell, the final cost;
The Judgment Seat of Christ, is for God's people … rewards gained
    or lost.

Nature

Beauty Here …
More Beauty Hereafter

(Villanelle)

The Heavens declare the glory of God,
And the firmament showeth His handiwork;
On a beautiful earth dwells man of the sod.

Even midst sin's destruction, beauty does lurk.
Air perfumed by lilacs, purple and white …
Cascading the air – senses alert.

Sun's rays on lake makes water reflect bright,
Tree lined mirrored banks standing straight and tall;
Without brush a "nature picture" brought to light.

Bird songs in the trees on ears softly fall …
Except for the "mockingbird," each sings its song
By rote … not listening to the other's call.

Rosebuds replace the flowers that have gone.
Petals fall in a shower around the base …
Fragrance lingers after last rose has shown.

God not only gave man a beautiful place,
But, sent His own Son to die in our stead;
Applied to a heart, Christ's blood does sin efface.

It's by grace through faith … and to works not wed,
Salvation is a gift … lest any man should boast.
It's of the Spirit … of the Spirit led.

The first Heaven is where birds fly,
Sun, moon and stars are in the Second Heaven.
Third Heaven's where dwells the Heavenly host.

To live with Christ for aye … when life is done
After millions of years … life's just begun!

The Apple

The apple, be it … green – yellow or ruby-
    red –
So many different textures – mellowed or
    green …
Tartness … sweetness, varied as a variety
    is seen;
Trees, young, some old, and twisted, some of the limbs …
    dead.
Apples to eat or apples to dice … apples for
    butter or apples for pies …
Nutmeg and cinnamon with apples goes …
    nice …
Many dishes with apples to please the
    appetite …
Apples, a good food – for old or young or those
    on a diet;
Apples so delicious, could have been the fruit in Eve's day;
Eat alone … going on your way.
Hmm … in a pie – delicious "al a mode" or cheddar
    on the side;
Pork chops – with apples, a few onions …
    following the cooking guide …
Lots of truth … proven at last – to help keep the
    doctor away … an apple a day!

The Winter's Moon

(Rondeau)

Mounds of ice seem to shroud the winter's moon;
When ice covers the ground, the sun's a boon;
If this heat could be saved … put away safe …
Get rich in winter months … not just assumed;
The global warming … on the news' screen would boom!

Go get your sunscreen, shades and hat, and don't fume;
Many summer days on the horizon loom …
Just think winter … icicles, gracing the leaves;
Mounds of ice sent to shroud the winter's moon.

Sun's so hot now, but winter's coming;
A sunny vacation spot … and pay for a room!
If imagination's good, you may start to freeze;
Don't be dismayed so soon … it's only June;
Mounds of ice seem to shroud the winter's moon.

Fog

Fog obscures the pathway . . .
     the freeways and roads . . .
It keeps the traveler from seeing far into the
     distance – as he would;
Still continuing to press forward on his journey
     to some other destination or to his abode –;
Lights always blindingly bright with visibility only a few feet
. . .
     not turning back – yet, perhaps he should.

Yet, in life . . . in the living of it – man wants
     all the answers . . . laid at his feet –
Faith is trusting the Lord; letting Him in His
     wisdom guide – yet, lead;
More dangerous the misty fog that obscures
     the intersection where two roads or highways meet . . .
God, Who knows all, sees all – is everywhere at
     the same time . . . yet man is finite – God has decreed.

Waiting

Waiting through winter for the spring;
Watching as snowflakes fall …
How much more snow and ice there'll be;
Before the robin's call.

Sitting by the fire is cozy …
Popping corn … roasting nuts –
While longing for spring's first, "posy";
When the birds sing and strut.

Time yet … before winter's cloak folds;
So enjoy what you can …
Icicles and snow … wind and cold;
Hot chocolate … on demand!

Waiting for Spring

Waiting through winter for the spring;
When snow melts and birds sing …
Crocuses come peeping through the grass;
Warm sun … gone winter's sting.

New leaves are sighted on the trees;
Little buds in view …
Butterflies and bees fan the breeze;
Grass wet …with drops of dew.

Bright morning sun, to start the day;
New energy seems to flow …
To work or school … each, on his way;
Laughter is heard … as they go.

There is much beauty in winter;
Outlines sculptured in snow …
Icicles cover trees of fir –
Spectacular … winter show.

Staying inside does get on nerves;
Spring … everyone adores …
All God's creation … seems to stir;
Comes alive …whole outdoors.

Springtime … glorious season of the year;
Creation … comes awake …
Four seasons nice … but, springtime's dear;
Fishing dates … on the lake.

In evenings, after work and school,
At twilight of the day …
Breaking away … from winter's rule;
Lingering … in moonlight's way.

How Does Your Garden Grow?

Such beauty of spring surrounds,
Flowers all colors and hues;
Seeds planted ... now they cover,
Green grass still wet with dew.

Trees with branch and leaf so dense,
Baring only spots of blue ...
Birds singing, but can't see whence,
Much chattering, as birds will do.

Mountains rise in the distance
Covered with all shades of green;
Blue canopy, they enhance ...
Beauty in the flowing streams.

God made the earth beautiful;
But, does it reach deep inside?
Bringing beauty to one's life;
Spirit buoyed ... life's fray benign.

God remains close ... ever near
To those who remain with Him;
Draw close to Him; have no fear;
Those who do ... He draws nigh to them.

Christ gives beauty to the heart,
Where there's a continual feast;
A beautiful garden ... a flower mart,
Where a bouquet's the very least.

Thoughts we feed on, is what we plant;
Heaven's precept, "path" is straight:
Study and prayer give a new slant,
Repentance … sweeps clean the slate.

If you're sad, God knows to start;
He needs no one to inform …
Where He is, He sees the heart;
Whether happy or forlorn.

Yet, He waits for us to come …
Lean upon His loving arm;
Our weakness, in faith turning from:
A child secure … from ALL alarm.

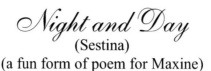
Night and Day
(Sestina)
(a fun form of poem for Maxine)

The sun came up shining so bright,
On the starting time for the day;
Slowly drifting in its own path,
Warming with zest, reaching the west;
Leaving behind the good it's done;
Hiding self, not dooming the moon.

Earth's nightlights are the stars and moon,
Their soft light is muted, not bright;
They fade from sight when night is done,
All have their watch in space of day;
Not to intrude as sun goes west …
Keeping vigil in their right paths.

During day, the sun sails its paths;
Signs and seasons fill sun and moon;
Sun, stars, and moonlight east and west,
With warmth and light at times so bright;
Sun bright, moonlight almost as day,
Moon's many cycles … not outdone.

Sun not turned … when cloud's drifting done;
Though obscured by clouds, stayed its path;
East to west, its schedule each day –,
Never changes, as does the moon …
From half and quarter to full bright,
Regularly setting in its place west.

What glorious sunsets in the west,
Beautiful colors when day's done;
Perhaps subdued … sometimes bright red,
Dark, white, or rosy clouds on path …
Sun moving, making way for moon;
As night creeps in at end of day.

Must work, yet, get some sun each day,
Sun lights – the north, south, east and west;
Waiting sunset, then light of moon …
Moonlight and starlight … when sun's done;
Fragrant flowers strewn along life's path,
Bringing to earth's site … beauty bright.

Bright sunshine warms our summer days;
Warm winter's cold path … east to west;
Sun's work done, we look for the moon.

We Wait, But, the Roses Won't

(A Ghazal)

As I sit looking across the lake from my backyard.
I see trees growing upside down on the far side bank.

Lily pads cover a portion of the shallow part at the right
    end of the lake.
The turtles perch on old stumps and lie in the sun to bake.

The little flat bottom boat is resting upside down.
When children and grandchildren get here, it will move
    around.

Fishing from the boat is a part of their vacation fun.
All have grown tired by end of day, at setting of the
    sun.

As my eyes focus closer to the house where I on my lounger
    sit,
There's the big shade trees covering the picnic area …
    with grandchildren, always a hit.

Meals outside are a part of our summertime agenda.
We'll have wiener roasts and barbeque ribs so very tender.

Flowers are beginning to bloom in their containers spaced
    there.
The picnic area, though shaded, isn't left bare.

The two swings are still, awaiting those little feet,
    who get such a thrill.
They'll be running, jumping, playing … getting their fill.

The little pink roses are finally blooming close by the
    picnic tables.
They won't wait or last long … need enjoy them while one's
    able.

Even the lizards return to the shade, after an excursion
    on a bug raid.
The sun, though hot, is healing … another benefit for man,
    God has made.

The rooster crows as helicopters fly overhead.
He brings to our notice, … though hot, he isn't dead.

My daughter just left for the house … leaving her lounger
    empty.
Maxine, "a Ghazal" is about what surrounds … stop!
    You've already written … more than what you see!

Beneath the Surface

Plants don't grow only above the ground …
   tendrils reaching down to circle around;
That's where life for the plant hangs
   in the balance…;
Sunshine and rain push the plant's
   roots on down.
A lease on life … a network of roots
   reaching for nutrients, every ounce.

The same proves true as lives are
   lived on earth …
You see what's above ground, yet, time will tell of the
   strength of roots to be found …
Faith in the Lord and trust go hand in hand –
   courage and strength of man may come from birth.
The showing made for all to see … comes
   forth from roots by which we're bound.

Quiet

It's quiet … while really isn't …
Hearing sounds, but in the distance –;
Spirit and heart are soothed in the sun;
While wind ripples the water's resistance.

Shadows play upon tree in light,
Butterflies hovering where flowers begin –;
Wind blowing leaves out of sight.
As warmth of sun's rays softly descend.

All noise suspended, not coming near,
The quiet soothes the spirit – closer to God,
But, out and away, many things to hear
No concern to me … as head begins to nod.

Oh! To live with spirit and body at one;
Living close to God through Christ, His Son;
Is the nearest to Heaven on earth to be done,
Until we 're in Heaven, and earth's race is run.

Quiet … yet, if you listen – not really quiet.
If you listen to what surrounds –
Birds, crickets, chickens and bees … what a riot;
When your heart's on thinking
   thoughts, can override outward sound.

Softly

The wind blowing softly …;
As wind chimes play a tinkling tune;
Music playing by the breeze … yet lofty –;
While the music wafts toward the moon.

A soft whisper … floating on the air …;
Crickets and tree frogs – seemingly far away;
Noises drifting in a tide to hear,
Yet, contained in the area to stay.

In the distance … softly the rain …
Is heard to bend with a soft wind;
As it approaches … the country lane –;
Raindrops softly … descend.

The earth is bathed with the soft shower of rain …
With the ground slowly absorbing as it falls;
Droplets splashing, dripping, down the windowpane,
Softly on the air, is carried the night bird's call.

Busy, Busy, Busy!

After the rain which was needed,
The noise of tractors and mowers
Is heard while gardens are weeded;
Root cellars readied for storage.

Weather will change to winter soon;
Like the bear … mowers hibernate …
Until spring when growing time looms,
All grass cutters will rest and wait.

In God's plan, He made the seasons;
There's something unique to each one,
Liking one best isn't treason …
God's Handiwork lacking in none!

The Butterfly

The butterfly is beautiful!
Colors of the rainbow seen
As if prisms reflecting light
When water and sun are teemed.

Blowing air bubbles of soap
At which children love to play,
Sun making little rainbows
Like butterflies, they don't stay.

God made such awesome beauty
First an egg, then caterpillar,
The pupa, then the adult ...
Caterpillars are destructive killers.

God's power is seen in this change.
Pollen is carried by butterflies,
So flowers can make fruit and seed,
All planned by a God so wise.

Butterflies differ so much;
Three-eighths to nine-inch wingspread,
Wings of assorted colors ...
Hard to see in a flowerbed.

Butterflies blend with flowers,
Adding beauty while feeding,
Helpful, as they have no teeth,
Carrying pollen when retreating.

God, Who made the butterflies,
Certainly knows each one of us.
Anytime, can call our name …
Man should in the Saviour trust.

The butterfly is beautiful!
Colors of the rainbow seen,
As if prisms reflecting light,
When water and sun do teem.

Summertime

So many memories of summer's past;
A favorite place, the ol' swimming hole.
Waiting for this – time didn't go fast.
Carrying lunch sack and fishing pole;
So anxious to be off – with new line to cast.
It matters not if the catch be perch or bass!

Water flowing in the lively creek,
Flowers in profusion along the bank;
Much alive in summer, in winter so bleak!
An old crossing made with rock and plank.
Such balmy air of honeysuckle did reek.

A wild rosebush – my favorite flower – breaking rank!
With jeans rolled up and barefoot feet;
A place to picnic then on the ground to sink;
This is just a peek of living at its best.
All the birds singing as if in contest.
Fascinating to watch them fly to their own little nest.
Such relaxing fun – a summertime fest!

Summertime abundance so filled with fun;
Nights with big moon and star-filled sky.
Days drenched in light, a canopy, the sun;
So much to do – tell the blues good-bye!
Chores must be done, but do them on the run;
After that – what next? – must decide – oh, my!

A cookout in evening, at close of day;
Fresh things from the garden, a specialty.
Everyone helping and getting in the way;

As long as summer lasts, it will ever be;
So much going on – not a minute free,
But, the best time of year — always to me!

In evening, after the day is spent;
After supper – sitting under the trees;
Talking, singing, chattering over all the events;
Listening to the noise of crickets and bees.
Enjoying this as long as you can – makes sense!
Outdoors in your own backyard – it costs no fees!

At dusk, flowers blooming, all over the place;
Spilling over beds, urns, walkways, too.
Children playing games, liking to race;
Hiding from everyone, and then saying, "Boo!"
Play clothes, in order – no Sunday lace!
Tumbling and playing as happy children do!

After farm animals are watered and fed;
The chickens to roost – the cows will "moo!"
Then to sit on feed trough painted red;
Laughing and talking, as people will do.
Until it's way past time to be in bed;
Dreaming in the twilight – stars so bright – fireflies too!

But, the Calendar and Almanac?

Hard to plan an early garden ... with the weather
    changing so,
You can never tell if there'll be ... rain, hail, sleet
    or snow!
Seems it's time ... looking at calendar and almanac – the usual
    things by which we go;
Waiting for weather report ... hopefully - sunshine and
    rain ... anything other – a gardener's foe.

The date on calendar and almanac so stated ... time to plant –
    with garden tools so aided;
Plants are in ... tomatoes, peppers, cabbages ... that's just to begin,
Seeds put in rows later ... careful to plant where last year ...
    something different had been –;
Each year ... with gardening, it's never the same – only the
    anticipation and expectation abide.

Much ado ... when the news reports say ... "Hail is on its way" ...;
Hurrying and scrambling ... for jars - the lot, without delay ...
    plants must be covered night or day;
Sometimes it seems best to just forget ... making a garden and do
    what many do ... or say.
Yet, each year ... when springtime is near ... enthusiastically
    heading for the garden with renewed zest!!

In gardening for sure ... one is made to know and plainly see —;
It's the Lord, our God, who controls the elements that be.
The more ... "acu" the weather report becomes ... it has always
    seemed to me;
The further off the prediction ... for God just lets us see —
    control and change of weather is up to Him, not us.

Earth's Sounds

Listen ... so many sounds seep through, when one thinks it's
    quiet;
When obvious sounds have all faded away ...;
Traffic ...with machinery's noise – gone from the day –;
At first, one is lulled to think ... all noise is held at bay.

Moving away from where louder noise does lay ...;
We're capable of hearing that ... which does stay –;
At first elusive ... then gradually many sounds, we do hear;
As we listen more closely to that ... that's near.

The breeze blowing softly ... fluttering the leaves ...;
Tall pines whispering, as the wind through needles weave –;
Ripened grain swaying, twisting, bending in a shower of rain;
Small animals scampering, scurrying across the lane.

The meandering brook rushing swiftly over stones, as it flows;
Singing a trickling, tinkling tune wherever it flows –;
Such, "quiet" ... soothing to the nerves ... yet, sound nonetheless;
With a quiet spirit ... one listens and hears the best.

Insects buzzing, zinging, chitchatting their song ...;
Though singing together ... a different song – while marching along;
Birds singing in unison or alone ... their own inherited tune –;
Coyotes or wolves howling ... looking at the moon.

A soft drizzling rain ... dripping off the trees ...;
Such a comforting sound ... yet, quiet waters flow into raging seas.
Earth's varied and wonderful sounds ... when taking time to note;
Point everyone to a great God ... Who isn't remote.

To be completely in harmony with nature, means to be at one
    with God;
By accepting His Son, Jesus ... the earth, His creation, for we
    are of the sod.
Observe the earth's sounds ... when you think you're away from it all;
If you only listen ... there are many sounds – though different
    from the mall!

In Time (Gardening)

The rain came … just in time …
To sprout the seeds – every kind.

Fall gardens are much more fun …;
Not so many weeds – the garden overrun.

If frost comes early – or very late …
With a garden of greens – doesn't matter the date.

God gives the sunshine and rain;
Our gardens grow – as God's blessing flow.

No matter if experienced gardener or not –;
The weather – has no favorites – mattering not a jot.

If God doesn't bless the work that is done;
Just a lot of wasted time, in heat of the sun.

Gardening time, we get everything ready …;
Such excitement … even the air is heady.

We watch to see when the little seeds sprout;
After awhile – we gather garden tools and are digging about.

Vegetables all kinds – from gardens of our own;
Seem so much better … than ordering by phone.

Everyone should have of earth a little plot;
To grow vegetables – an enjoyment that's man's lot.

Doctrinal

and

Didactic

Courage

You are indeed blessed, if you are privileged to
  know one of courage ...
Not thinking of self ... but, for right, with faith,
  stands bold;
One who doesn't hide ... crouching, as it were in
  cowardice, as a bird in a covered cage –;
With faith and God's Word as the base ... one can
  never fold.

Courage is going ahead when something is right ...
  when the majority withdraws;
Knowing that you and God are a majority in any –
  crowd ...
Man can never successfully overrule what is God's
  unerring law.
Humility is companion with faith and courage ...
  not with pride and arrogance, proud.

Age doesn't matter ... one doesn't have to grow old
  before standing for right ...
Faith should increase as one does age ... for then
  they're able to look back –
Recall examples they've seen ... how God provided
  strength and light in right's fight.
Courage comes from God ... in trust and faith, an
  area – where so many lack.

Forgiveness

God's Word is like unto a mirror;
In which everyone needs to look.
And examine with utmost care,
Our heart – each cranny – every nook!
Not liking what's lurking there …
To hide from the truth – we're not to brook.
Each person responsible – sin to rout!
The devil will deceive by hook or crook!
Faith in Christ will turn a life about.
But, we become weak when we doubt!

If when searching through our heart;
We find to others we've been unkind.
For they did us wrong; from the start.
If we would be forgiven … mind;
Honestly – we must forgive – God drew the line!
For with whatsoever judgment we render;
We will be judged by God – in kind.
Though to Christ our hearts we surrender;
Confessing our sins in repentance – not falling behind;
Staying close to God – forgiveness – keeps hearts tender!

Reaping What You Sow

As you know – you reap what you sow,
You certainly reap later than you sow!
You reap more than you sow.
Nice to know – we can choose what we sow.

Plant a garden; plan as you would.
The ground be prepared, or should.
It takes sunshine and rain;
Sometimes working with inflicted pain.

In our lives, it's the same;
Reaping what we sow – life's no game.
Others will be affected, no doubt;
We need be careful what we're about.

Christ is always our help;
The Bible tells he cleansed the lepers.
Faith in Christ helps with our sowing,
As down life's rows we keep going.

What we sow affects many others,
Not only ourselves – our brothers.
We need sow to the spirit;
And not to the flesh – there's merit.

Have Unstaggering Faith

"Draw nigh unto Me, saith the Lord,
And I will draw nigh unto thee."
Distance between ... with sin is marred;
Ultimately, a choice for you and me!

When cares of life fill space between,
Pushing the Lord farther away ...
His Word tells us on Him to lean;
To be happy, we must obey.

"Be of good courage ... and He will
Strengthen thine heart," ... so states His Word!
Courage fills a heart that's strong in faith,
Trusting ... in life, with God's truth girt.

There was Daniel in the lion s' den ...
For his faith, God delivered him;
Three Hebrew children ... faithful men,
From the fiery furnace, God saved them.

God kept David from his enemies ...
David repented ... when he sinned;
Was kept as apple of God's Eye ...
No harm can come when God defends!

Abraham, by faith obeyed God.
To sacrifice, Isaac, his son;
God provided the ram instead
His faith proved ... as if deed was done.

Enoch pleased God three hundred sixty-five years,
And was not ... before God took him;
He walked with God, staying near ...
He lived faith midst what was grim.

Moses chose rather to suffer ...
Afflictions with children of God;
Rather than enjoy sin's pleasures
For a season ... choice prevalent in sod.

There was not another like Job,
Trusting God in his infirmities ...
God blessed him more after his woes;
His suffering seemed an eternity.

Elijah left in a whirlwind ...
God gathered him home without fail;
Faith caused him upon God to depend,
Refuting the prophets of Baal.

It's up to you ... the choices you make;
While we still live and have our being ...
Not resisting 'till death doth take
In flight ... spirit from body freeing.

Mordecai, by faith, advised Esther,
She trusted God to save the Jews;
Hamen was hanged on the gallows
Built for Mordecai ... such news!

"God works in mysterious ways His
Wonders to perform" ... we must trust;
Without faith it's impossible ...
To please God ... for to please God ... faith is a must!

Did You Know?

(Proverbs 17:22) (2 Samuel 23:39)

"A merry heart doeth
Good like a medicine …"
"Happy is the man who
Does not condemn himself
In that … he alloweth."

Did you know effectual …
Fervent prayer of righteous
Man, availeth much? … True!
Stay close to God … a must.

Who lives … immoral life …
There's a curse that never leaves …
Best to follow God's laws,
Purity won't deceive …

Decisions made when young,
Follow rest of our days …
Take time to think and pray
For consequences do stay.

We can ask forgiveness,
But, pay for deeds we must …
Though David did repent …
For Bathsheba … did lust.

Baby did not live long.
Nor consequence to hide,
Not long before 'twas gone,
Urriah had to die.

Best to obey God's Will ...
Chastisement not severe;
Hearts will be spirit-filled,
Close to God, without fear.

Grow Up!

Parents are responsible for their children ...
    duty bound!
Small children – just growing up, are the
    most easily led.
Some parents, instead of leading – it seems –,
    vie for the generations, turned around!
Only play at being adults ...want to be
    irresponsible children instead!
Strong moral values, trusting the Lord – facing
    life thus ... on solid ground!
When parents try turning their role about,
    it's quite disconcerting!
An adult ... when in their thinking and actions
    ... immaturity is found;
There's complete disregard for reliability –,
    discounting its worth.
Ignoring troubles – they won't diminish ...
    they only mound –
So sad! – To be an adult and responsibility as,
    "NIL," as a few years from birth –
Children need someone, to direct their lives,
    who's sound.
There seems to be such deficiency ... you could
    say there's a dearth!!

Or Would You Rather Be a Pig?!

A fair woman without discretion is like jewel
    in a swine's snout …
Without the Lord, one returns to the wallowing in
    the mire.
Though washed and tied with ribbons, a pig to the first mud
    hole…
        he'll find the shortest route.
Not self-righteousness, but Salvation will
    change heart's desire.

God's people are to be peculiar for God to
    be around …
Demeanor and dress are to be different
    from lost of the world.
So others can see God in their lives
    to surprise and astound;
The lost look on God's children to see if a
    difference can be found.

God's plan for saving the lost is by faith,
    accepting His Son,
Works that remain after they are tried by
    fire are for rewards …
Salvation is free … Christ died on the cross
    for everyone;
Chastisement … loss of rewards await those who turn
    from the Lord.

What If?

What if the Apostle Paul had
    wavered in his faith …
Would he have been accounted worthy
    in the Bible to occupy such a space?
What if when in prison, he would
    have been depressed –;
Instead of singing God's praises … deep in
    depression, he did wrest.

What if when God called upon
    Abraham to offer Isaac – he had refused?
What if when he was called upon to
    leave the Ur of the Chaldees – no travel ensued.
Abraham wouldn't have been called the father
    of a great nation
His lack of faith would have
    lowered his station.

What if John the Baptist had failed to answer
    God's call –
To preach the gospel … as upon repentant
    hearts it did fall …
People came out from the cities to the
    wilderness … to see and hear the man,
Who bellowed like a bull with boldness, preaching
    repentance, for the Kingdom of God is at hand.

What if Joseph … when sold in Egyptian
    bondage had deserted the Lord?
Instead of during the famine … saving
    his family and nation whom he adored;

What depended upon Joseph was
   his relationship to God …
God used Joseph to save his people …
   by his faith … though of the sod.

What if we tried serving the Lord with
   all our heart …
What if when God's work was to be done,
   we couldn't wait to start;
Think what the world would be … if
   everyone who professed a child of God to be,
Would by faith … step out on God's
   promises … what a change the world would see.

What if so many others … examples
   to us all …
Had failed the test to perform some
   service when God upon them did call?
History records many faithful even unto death, besides
   ones we read about in God's Word …
To help us as God's children learn …
   our own will ... not God's to spurn.

What if Job had been depressed … had given
   up the fight?
With his so-called "friends" … giving
   advice … chiding – making light –;
God said to satan concerning Job …
   "There is none like him in the earth."
The patience of Job is a lesson to all –
   tribulation worketh patience – not given at birth.

What if Christ had called for more than
    twelve legions of angels instead of dying on the Cross?
If He had called them, what about
    our salvation – could we have stood the loss?
He was obedient unto the Father even
    unto death … Salvation's door –
Seeing how they loved us … we should
    love them more.

Are You Ready?

Many times, we've been asked, "Are you ready?"
Numerous times, we've asked the same …
When death comes knocking at the doors;
Excuses will be lame.

Need be prepared, ready to go;
Without a moment's notice …
For death may sneak up like a foe;
Or torturing, goad us.

Christ died for all; Salvation's free,
By grace through faith, we're saved;
When we've been saved, the soul's ready;
Though body lies in grave.

Behold now's the day of Salvation,
Now's the accepted time …
No excuses, there can be none;
Are you ready? … is prime!

Death

From the beginning, death begins to creep,
Stretching toward the grave, long as there's life;
The law of nature, all life, death does meet;
Whatever lives, will die; the proof is rife.

Death may leap, or take slowly to the grave;
Times of escape, with another time wrought,
This is man's lot, born in sin and depraved;
Whether sudden, or a long battle fraught.

Sting of death is sin, strength of sin the law;
"Death where is thy sting, grave where is thy victory?"
It's through Christ; we're presented without fault,
Time's wasting … and we'll soon be, as we'll be.

Matters not the vehicle … used in death;
Behold, now, is the day of Salvation …
Preparing for death in life isn't a myth;
Eternity's die is "cast," at life's setting sun!

Yes, as the tree falleth, so shall it lie …
For the jaws of death … hold its victims fast;
Paramount is, not when … but, HOW we die;
Repentance and faith in Christ removes the past.

Sins are removed as far as east from west,
When with the heart we accept Christ as Saviour;
Oh, with how great a Saviour … man is blessed;
Absent the body, present with the Lord, at death.

The Heart of Things

Life of the body's in the blood;
Heart is body's pump …
Has much to do … if health is good;
As heart works in the trunk.

The heart of man … is busy, too;
As seat of our affections …
The Bible tells us this is true;
Heart's work is never done.

"As a man thinketh in his heart;"
God's Word says, … "so is he …"
Of the heart's abundance … man speaks;
A window ALL can see.

For by grace through faith, we're saved;
Repentance … is the need …
Christ died on Calvary – sin to waive,
If we'll only believe.

So many things … in Holy Writ;
Concerns the heart of man …
It's deceitful … who can know it;
God does, and understands.

Nothing hid from a great God's view;
Man's heart's an open book …
Conversation … tells me and you;
LISTENING … is like a LOOK.

Man's relationship to the Lord;
Has to start with the heart …
Choose the Lord … not a life that's marred;
Choosing … is each one's part.

Salvation's a gift … NOT by WORKS:
No work will make us worthy …
The devil … close to each one lurks;
Of the earth, we're earthy.

Desire of heart makes the difference;
Trusting the Lord or not,
We need guard our hearts now … and hence;
Trust God's Word … every jot.

Determination is Rife!

In the Bible – in the Book of Ruth – remember
 Naomi's daughter-in-law... Ruth?
To Naomi - Ruth was a true friend – ready to
 share the hardships Naomi saw.
In Genesis ...we read of another instance ...
 the very opposite – of a truth.
Rebekah and Isaac were sorely troubled about
 their daughter-in-law;
At the end of chapter twenty-seven – in the
 book of Genesis – to despair reduced!
Easu took to wife of the daughters of Heth in
 the land of Canaan;
He was forty years old ... should have had better
 judgment – not easily seduced!
Rebekah said to Isaac – "I'm weary of my life,
 because of the daughters of Heth."

Esau's marriage was a grief of mind to Isaac
 and Rebekah – in reading, it's easy to see.
If Jacob, the other son – takes a wife such as
 these, which are of the daughters of the land;
Rebekah lamented to Isaac, ..."What good shall my
 life do me?"
Isaac blessed Jacob – gave him a charge – sent him
 away ... following their plan ...;
They sent him from Canaan to Padan-Aram ... to his
 Mother's father – Bethuel;
To find a wife in a different land – where lived
 his kin; they didn't ban.
Isaac and Rebekah sent Jacob away ... they were
 adamant in their refusal.
As parents they saw the need of taking a stand ...
 their attitude –"Do what we can!"

Rebekah and Isaac with legitimate concern – for
    Jacob – sent him with relatives to stay;
Though he didn't marry of the daughters of the
    land of Canaan.
His uncle, Laban, tricked him concerning the wife he
    chose … twice he did pay.

Leah was his wife – for Rachel he had to pay double to
    make her his wife – working as he could.
When they were moving, Rachel took her "false gods"
    … and on the camel they lay.
It mattered not how far away Jacob went … God was
    over all the land.
God, at times, overrides situations to work His will –
    Jacob was father of Israel's twelve tribes.
The name "Jacob" means trickster – it seems left to
    himself – he was headlong, once and again!

What type of daughter-in-law would you make or
    choose …?
Ruth, or the daughters of Heth, of the land of
    Canaan?
Daughter-in-laws have a choice to what they …
    will do.
As a daughter-in-law … do you serve God or
    mammon?
You can have the attributes of Naomi's
    daughter-in-law, Ruth … it's up to you,
Or be like the daughter of Heth of the land of
    Canaan – spirit like that of Haman.
If yielding our lives to the will of Christ … and
    right, we pursue – we'll be as Ruth …
A blessing to mother and father-in-law, yea, to
    all … when selfishness turns to love!

Old is Forever New!

Some preachers may lay claim to the "old school",
Others are proud to say they're of the "new".
The "new" is "old" if cutting straight God's word;
The "old" is "new" when the Gospel is heard.

Though there were some who said they were of "Paul,"
While others said they were of "Apollos".
'Tis God who provides and gives the increase;
Realizing this … it seems strife should cease!

Both old and new … God's word forever true:
Holding Biblical truths doesn't promise fame;
God's preachers, with others, must answer to Him,
Jealousy is cruel as the grave … so grim!

Salvation's by grace through faith … not by works;
When believing "works" in the heart pride lurks;
It was Christ who died on the cross to save the lost.
Man is born in sin and depraved.

Preach the word, … "Be instant in season and out;"
To please God there must be faith without doubt;
Remove not the ancient landmarks that thy father's have set.
God's word remains the same.

Talents and abilities are gifts from God;
Why exalt thyself … Oh, man of the sod!
Unprofitable servants … after we've done
All it's our duty to do … that is All not just one!

Identify with the "Old School" or "New"?
All honor and glory to God is due!!!
(Proverbs 22:28)

God Knew Us Before and After

(Psalm 139:15,16 and Jeremiah 1:5

When we were curiously wrought in the earth,
To God, our substance was not hid before birth;
Only His Eyes knew and saw our being,
Being imperfect ... brought together at once.

All our members in Thy book were written,
And which in continuance were fashioned,
When as yet, unseen, there was none of them,
We were fashioned and embroidered by Him.

God ordained Jeremiah to be a prophet,
Before he was born, God's own plan was set;
God sanctified him while still in the womb,
A great work for his future in life did loom.

God knew each of us before we were born,
Before in the womb even ... we were formed;
As God knew us then ... He also knows us now,
Looking into each heart .. . if to God it bows.

When did the clay say to the potter, "Nay?"
Since God is the potter and we are the clay:
Are there any who dare to plead his case?
But, instead by faith, ask mercy and grace!

The Lord's Church

When Jesus walked the shores of Galilee …
Called out His Apostles who were the first church;
John the Baptist, preached the same message as He,
John prepared the materials for the Lord's church.

John the Baptist preached, Salvation through Christ;
In the wilderness … bellowed like an ox!
He preached so all could hear and understand;
Repent! … The Kingdom of Heaven's at hand.

Salvation comes through Christ, and not by works;
Repentance and faith's the Way, Christ is the DOOR.
Seems the mind of man is forever irked …
Will not accept Christ, the Door; … he wants more!

Salvation doesn't come by works … all of GRACE;
The Lord's Church has no part with the Nicolaitanes;
"Preacher," rule over "laity" … has no space;
Saved by grace, rulers none … all just God's sons.

When God calls a preacher, he's not his own;
Only an under-shepherd … of the Lord …
Christ, the Good Shepherd, never condones wrong;
Those who serve, office well … receive rewards.

They're not to rule over God's heritage,
Rulers, they're not to be … they have no place;
Though most members SHARE, same lineage as he;
In many instances … this is the case!

Question is … to whom does the Church belong?
Is it the Lord's, or members on its rolls?
If the Lord's … then His doctrine should be strong!
Purpose of Lord's Church … SALVATION OF SOULS!!!

Gifts of God – Not Man

God in His Wisdom and great love for the human
    race;
Placed man it the beautiful Garden of Eden that
    was his space.
But, Adam and Even forfeited all their privileges –
    life a different pace.
After this, God's Grace was available and everything
    wasn't a waste.
Though Adam and Even were driven from Eden having to
    leave in haste!
No more would they talk with God in the garden,
    because of sin and disgrace.

God still loving His sinful, rebellious and fallen
    creation;
Sent Christ, His only begotten Son, to provide our
    Salvation.
Christ died at Calvary … though crucified, it was
    of His own volition.
He could have called ten thousands of angels, but
    this was His mission.
All who accept the Son God sent, are reborn and will have
    a new body in the resurrection.
To live in a mansion, He has gone to prepare for all
    who accept His redemption.

God not only loved the human race with the giving of
    His Son …
Look around and you will see all the earthly pleasures,
    freely given you and me.
We have the sky with all – its day and nighttime
    magic.

All parts of the world have different, beautiful
   attractions; not enjoying them is tragic.
The desert with all the cactus in bloom, a beautiful
   sight to see.
Loving the desert – this is true – at least to me …
   you feel so free.

To see all the Wonders of the World, people travel
   land and sea.
When in the place they reside – perhaps there's more
   beauty – there that be.
Oceans with gigantic waves and the tide are a
   magnificent sight.
There are places with woods, mountains, valleys, lakes,
   creeks and the like.
Not made by man – if he had, he wouldn't have done it
   right.
Trees man didn't plant, glowing in the fall, from red
   to gold, all colors bright.
With dogwood blooming on hills in the …
   spring.
All colors of green on the hillside and in valleys
   seen.
Even though Eden was lost, God gave us a place where
   beauty is keen.
Listening to politicians – I do believe – if some could
   claim – they – not God ordered this, our domain.
Remember this, we answer to God – what we are and what
   we vote – in this we'll be to blame!
God's blessings are not, "Pork Barrel" from Washington –
   they, too, are subject to … a God Who reigns!

Cinquains, Haiku, Senryu, Lunes, Sonnets and Triolets

Something New

(Triolet)

To some folks, what's new, always seems the best;
Bible remains the same … will never change …
There are some, who for God's truth won't digress.
To some folks, what's new, always seems the best;
Eagerly waiting, the old, to divest …
Multitudes caught up, when teachings are strange;
To some folks, what's new, always seems the best;
Bible remains the same … will never change.

No Place to Hide

(Triolet)

Man is never able to hide from God;
While that which hides God from man's, an idol!
Compared to God, man is a worm of the sod;
Man is never able to hide from God;
To exalt God is not considered mod …
Christ, as Savior, to the soul is vital!
Man is never able to hide from God;
While that which hides God from man's, an idol!

It's Priorities, Stupid!

(Triolet)

Love of money's, the root of ALL-evil:
Yet, there is no virtue in poverty!
It's priorities, stupid! … Young or feeble;
Love of money's, the root of ALL-evil:
Though has its place even midst God's people;
A medium of exchange is all it should be …
Love of money's, the root of ALL-evil:
Yet, there is no virtue in poverty!

True Values

Family values … we hear so much
    about …,
One family may value one thing – another
    some other –;
What's morally right … one should have
    without doubt;
The Bible, the basis and objective – search
    no further!

Forever Young

(Triolet)

Even though the outward man is perishing,
The inward man is being renewed day by day.
In salvation, … by grace through faith, Christ cherishing,
Even though the outward man is perishing,
Yet, younger inside, where the Spirit resides.
A renewed spirit, perpetual does stay.
Even though the outward man is perishing,
The inward man is being renewed day by day.
The renewed spirit, forever young will stay.

Fragile? Think Again

(Triolet)

Hurt feelings and tears come so easily,
With no provocation … cry for their way.
Taking the advantage with conniving …
Hurt feelings and tears come so easily,
Ruthless weapons on others used freely.
All not centered on them is held at bay,
Hurt feelings and tears come so easily,
With no provocation … cry for their way!

Our Daughter

(Triolet)

She's such a wonderful daughter!
On her we can depend!
No other would we prefer
She's such a wonderful daughter!
Obstacles to her never deter,
Her help she liberally does lend,
She's such a wonderful daughter!
On her we can depend.

For: Tena

So Many Things

(Triolet)

So many things I love to do!
To read, write, paint and cook
Those named are just a few!
So many things I love to do!
Always like learning something new!
At the beauty of nature I love to look,
So many things I love to do!
To read, write, paint and cook.

Memory Lane
(Sonnet)

Looking down memory lane where I have passed;
Standing on time's incline, thoughts looking back;
Much escaped the light and dark shadows cast …
Path lies straighter, now travel isn't lacked.
With much obscured … protection it can be;
Eyes not deterred from goal as summit seized;
Obstacles not deemed, or as none to see …
Meandering through as wind the leaves do tease.
Decisions alter many a life's path …
Trust in the Lord overcomes much danger:
Faith sails unhampered oe'r boulders and ravines;
Man's born to trouble and never a stranger.
    Faith sees the best route is letting God lead;
    With Him providing as He sees the need!

Upheld
(Sonnet)

Our faith in the Lord is our spirit's strength;
Discarded by many as not a force …
Always seeing what God can do … doubts relent;
God's Word and promises … our life's resource.
Though we all stumble and fall … must recall;
When Christ is ours … we're forever His –;
How can this be – so many times we face …
Alone, to be forever crushed … now strong.
Upheld in His Arms – protection assured;
T'was dust of the earth – from, which man was made.
Man's choice to make … man's choice our God endured.
For to be free to choose … Him to obey;
Glory is true … coming freely from You …
Obeying means glory … only a few.

A Fortunate Situation

(Cinquain)

Family …
You do not choose
Yet, some may prove the type
Friends … with qualities you would pick
By choice.

A Different Name

(Cinquain)

"Vacation" …
For some, means "work"
Must be done by others:
Who will grow more tired … remains to
Be seen.

End of School

(Triolet)

The whole school is in a turmoil!
End of school cleaning … once a year:
Test day couldn't allow to spoil!
The whole school is in a turmoil!
Outside to the inside a foil …
The halls are filled from there to here;
The whole school is in a turmoil!
End of school cleaning … once a year.

Which?

(Senryu)

depressed …
or could be lazy!
looks are same

Father's Day

(Triolet)

It's Father Day again this year
Love in hustle and bustle seen;
It's day to families that's dear,
It's Father's Day again this year
Visits, calls, cards … from far and near
Gifts and a feast fit for a king,
It's Father's Day again this year
Love in hustle and bustle seen.

You Never Knew Until Now

(Triolet)

Love, you never did know until now
Until you had children of your own.
Many times, on your knees you bow
Love, you never did know until now
Such love, you never did allow …
Then there are children of your bone,
You never did know until now
Until you had children of your own.

171

Dreamed?

(Cinquain)

I thought
I made apple
Fritters, and they numbered
Fourteen; when I came back! Had to
Have dreamed!

Sight-Seeing

(Cinquain)

Lounging
Basking in sun
Beautiful scenes of much
Visited places viewed as I turn
The page.

Repeat

(Cinquain)

What goes
'Round comes around
A circle has no end
Stopping off where it begins to
Go 'round.

Together
(Cinquain)

All for
One – one for all – A family ought to be
Support, encourage, correct, chasten,
With love.

Love in Action
(Cinquain)

God is
Love … but teaches
In His Word; an eye for
An eye … vengeance is mine saith …
The Lord.

In Its Own Time
(Cinquain)
Ecclesiastes 3:8

There is
A time to love,
And there's a time to hate;
There's a time of war, and a time …
Of peace.

Vengeance Belongs to God
(Cinquain)

Righteous
Indignation
Is not revenge … vengeance
Is mine saith the Lord and I will …
Repay!

Forward March
(Cinquain)

Scriptures
Say, "Be wise as
Serpents and harmless as
Doves" … God never has His people …
Retreat!

A Long Wait
(Cinquain)

Today …
Is Mother's Day
It comes only once a
Year: three hundred sixty-four … a
Long wait.

Above Par
(Cinquain)

No time!
Even with all
The modern appliances;
Slowed to what could be called … above
What's par.

Mother's Day
(Triolet)

Mother's Day I get many gifts;
Many things I like … some I need;
It's a good day with not a rift,
Mother's Day I get many gifts;
Best not into expectancy drift …
No disappointments there'll be to heed;
Mother's Day I get many gifts;
Many things I like … some I need.

No Time
(Triolet)

It seems today we have no time;
Even with modern technology …
Travel faster … conveniences combined;
It seems today we have no time;
It takes much longer to unwind …
Much, just let go … with an apology;
It seems today we have no time;
Even with modern technology.

Haiku

hurry
is what we hear
for what?

God So Loved

(Triolet)

God so loved the world
   He sent His Son to die
By Adam, the world into sin, was hurled.
God so loved the world
God's plan for redemption, in Christ unfurled,
   His death at Calvary, is where it lay
God so loved the world
   He sent His Son to die.

By Grace Through Faith

(Triolet)

By grace through faith we are saved,
   It's a gift of God and not by works
When accepting Christ as Saviour, our sin is waived.
By grace through faith, we are saved,
We're born in sin, our nature depraved!
   The devil's aim is to ruin lives, close he lurks.
By grace through faith we are saved,
It's a gift of God and not by works.

The Summer Sun

(Triolet)

The summer sun is sometimes too warm
    Yet, can be soothing and healing,
Too much at once can do much harm.
The summer sun is sometimes too warm
With no hat, in places, brings alarm.
    To be caught out a terrible feeling.
The summer sun is sometimes too warm
    Yet, can be soothing and healing.

The Evergreen

(Triolet)

The evergreen's the star of winter,
    Time now for budding flowering trees,
Into fall some will linger.
The evergreen's the star of winter,
Ice and snow to them no hindrance.
    When winds blow hard and there's a freeze
The evergreen's the star of winter,
    Time now for budding, flowering trees.

The Red Rose

(Triolet)

I pressed the red rose in a book,
    The one he gave to me.
I still can take a look,
I pressed the red rose in a book,
Laid it in its nook,
    It's there where I can see;
I pressed the red rose in a book,
    The one he gave to me.

Parents Are Responsible

(Triolet)

Parents are responsible for their children
    Not the country, state or village!
Parents should be protector, mentor, and friend.
Parents are responsible for their children
Children should know on them to depend,
    From very young or an older age.
Parents are responsible for their children
    Not the country, state or village!

Lies

(Triolet)

You hate those afflicted by your lies.
   The Lord hates a lying tongue.
To stay with the truth is wise
You hate those afflicted by your lies.
The truth, any refuting defies,
   Lies ruin a life, old or young,
You hate those afflicted by your lies.
   The Lord hates a lying tongue.

Difference in Work and Play

(Triolet)

Labor Day is a holiday …
Yet, so many people work!
Masses travel the highways;
Labor Day is holiday …
Leaving home to miss the fray,
Mind decides what's work or perk,
Labor Day is a holiday …
Yet, so many people work!

To Write a Sonnet

(Sonnet)

To write a sonnet ... where should I begin?
It isn't the theme ... at which I falter ...
But, what form does it take – many altered –;
It seems the form – not precise of other men.
Would it were allowed to ask them – explain;
Confusing ... where is the literary halter?
Although sincere ... sonnets not to palter.
All would-be students – rules don't disdain,
Wanting to learn ... rules to turn – must discern;
Ever to write ... going forward, not hindsight.
Trying ever so hard ... writing to learn.
Selecting custom rules – could be called bright.
Another time ... another era ... not to return.
A sonnet is a sonnet is a sonnet.

Same, Same

(Triolet)

Persons with opinions the same as ours,
Meet with favor and held in high esteem;
With them, we converse amicably for hours,
Persons with opinions the same as ours,
Intellect reaching mind's highest tower ...
Above all others, in thought it seems;
Persons with opinions the same as ours,
Meet with favor and held in high esteem.

West Texas

(Cinquain)

Hot sun
Not a cloud, just
Sun, no rain in sight
Wind blowing sand outside the house
Through cracks!

I Remember

(Cinquain)

Mud balls!
With a sprinkle
Of rain; is what you see …
In a sand storm … if you have clothes
On line.

One or More!

(Cinquain)

A steak
Supper tonight
Sounds wonderful to me
Salad, baked potatoes without or
With, "E"!

Referring to the Dan Quayle
incident with the spelling of "potato!"

Work Fast

(Cinquain)

With rain …
Grass grows so fast;
If mower doesn't hurry
The first to be mowed … will become
The last!

In Order

(Cinquain)

God's way
Is always best
Love, marriage, then children,
To nurture and admonish … in
The Lord.

It's Gold

(Cinquain)

Cane fields
Shimmer like gold,
As sun fills the breeze in
West Indies bringing owners delight
Like gold.

Quiet When Busy

(Cinquain)

The crow …
A noisy bird
Up from ground; darts flying
Busy pulling garden plants … no
Cawing.

Haiku

night sky …
shimmering with stardust
like dew

Haiku

a poem!
generic isn't
for me!

Senryu

the crow …
pulling up the corn is
never cawing

On Writing

(Triolet)

I would write better than I do:
Something inspiring to help man;
Reading God's Word helps one improve;
I would write better than I do:
Trying … shows excellence, I pursue;
Giving up … don't know if I can!
I would write better than I do:
Something inspirational to help man.

Senryu

a large inheritance …
friends, so many: until money's gone
friends joined enemies

Cart Before the Horse

(Cinquain)

Many
Priorities
Are misplaced, as self tops
The list … God and family are left …
Behind

Senryu

small package
tied prettily with ribbon
contains … self

Reaches Far
(Cinquain)

Package filled with
Self and tied with ego
Describes so much of human …
Nature

God's Will
(Cinquain)

The Lord
Can change the heart
Perspective's in order
Through repentance and faith with God's …
Will done

God's Love Turning to Hate
(Cinquain)

God's love …
Will turn to wrath
When cause is justified
And at man's derision our God …
Will laugh

In God's Care
(Cinquain)

The truth …
Will come to light
Surfacing in God's time
As we trust in the Lord and live
By faith

God's Perspective
(Cinquain)

God's Word …
Says a good name
Should be desired rather
Than riches … virtue's price above
Rubies

Dead End
(Cinquain)

When God's …
Love turns to hate
Laughter without mercy!
No place evil can flee from His
Presence

Keeping Time

(Cinquain)

Big Grandfather
Booms with chimes every hour
Awake on the hour … no sleep must …
Retire

Magnified

(Cinquain)

Package …
Is very small
Even adding ribbon
When all it contains is ego
And self!

On the Lord's Side

(Cinquain)

The Lord …
Says His grace is
Sufficient … He is a
Very present help in time of …
Trouble

Faith
(Cinquain)

Moses …
Led the children
Of Israel across the
Red Sea … dry land appeared when God …
Desired

God's Will
(Cinquain)

God will
Make a way for
His Will to be done and
Use us for His purpose when hearts …
Are right

God's Way
(Cinquain)

Prayer …
Sincere desire
Of the heart … without faith
It's impossible for us to …
Please God

Rest to Work

(Cinquain)

Work fast …
That we might rest
God's Word teaches work of
Our hands is part of enjoyment
Of life

Faith

(Cinquain)

"Thou canst
If Thou wilt" was
Statement of faith by one
Asking Jesus to heal him, a …
Leper

Senryu

a truck
couldn't see it
camouflaged

Actions Louder Than Words!

(Cinquain)

Void of conscience … deeds prove!
Evil eyes stream with tears
Gaining sympathy while planning …
Evil

Senryu

pristine white
it's covered with snow
garbage dump

Senryu

diamond encrusted
paved with faceted brilliance
sun on icy trees

Senryu

most weddings
the plan is forever
in dreams

Useless!

(Cinquain)

Doctor …
Gave good advice
His prescribed medicine
Didn't help, in one ear … out the
Other

Senryu

rain clouds today
been such a long dry spell
still missing the sun

Senryu

bad mood
like hair rinse with time …
wears off!

Senryu

be careful
good personality
same person

Haiku

sleet, ice, snow
white sparkling gems
water, slush, mud

Life

(Cinquain)

To dream
Or remember
Still amounts to the same
Thoughts of past and future … emerge
In mind

Lune

salvation through Christ
repentance
and faith come through Him

Lune

though family loves you
greater love
comes from God through Christ

Lune

birds have no lessons
songs pretty
man has to practice

Lune

in kitchen all day
fixing food
disappears so soon

Senryu

some people's faults
we easily see ... others we
camouflage

Pick and Choose

(Cinquain)

We see
What we want to
See ... by passing that we
Would rather not acknowledge ...
Ignore

193

Haiku

hurry have fun
snow is so soft and fluffy
the sun leaves mud

Just Cogitating!

(Triolet)

In a many category contest …
Hmmm … would more involvement, as chairman help?
Reach beyond "honorable mention," at best;
In a many category contest …
Such volume of entries, could prove a test:
To the understanding of contest depth;
In a many category contest …
Hmmm …would more involvement, as chairman help?

The Real One Please Stand

(Cinquain)

Will the
Inventor of …
The Internet please stand?
Reps. from the Pentagon stood, so …
Did AL!

What's the Final Answer?
(Triolet)

Now, just who did invent the Internet?
Al Gore says he did … reports say "Pentagon":
"News" said he's smart except on certain days;
Now, just who did invent the Internet?
It's decades old … Al would have been just a kid!
Hardly knowing Internet's pros and cons …
Now, just who did invent the Internet?
Al Gore says he did … report says "Pentagon".

A Must
(Cinquain)

Yes! Now!!!
Apologize …
Say what they want to hear!
For goodness' sake … please don't laugh … sound
Sincere!

Covetousness
(Triolet)

Covetousness is a terrible sin …
Consequence recorded in God's Word.
There can be no instance to defend.
Covetousness is a terrible sin …
Judgment awaits when God's wrath is stirred.
Wanting that illegal seems the trend.
Covetousness is a terrible sin …
Consequence recorded in God's Word.

Touch Not Mine Anointed

(Triolet)

The Lord said, "Touch not mine anointed and do
    my prophets no harm;"
God provides special care for those He has called
    to carry His Word.
One called to preach God's Word needs faith, and
    of the devil, be not alarmed.
The Lord said, "Touch not mine anointed and do my
    prophets no harm;"
He suffered no man to do them wrong:
    and yea, He reproved kings for their sake.
God said, His Word will be preached and
    to all quarters of the earth heard.
The Lord said, "Touch not mine anointed and do
    my prophets no harm;"
God provides special care of those He has called
    to carry His Word.

The Empty Tomb

(Cinquain)

Christ died
To save the lost
For God so loved the world …
Christ's resurrection left the tomb
Empty.

Christ Arose

(Cinquain)

For God …
So loved the world
Christ died to save the lost
On the third day Christ arose from
The grave.

Lune

no rain … it's so dry
then it rained!
water and mud slides

Lune

not hungry at all
so much food …
only morsels left

Lune

sunshine during day
moon and stars
are the light for night

Senryu

haircut …
hoped to look better
much worse

Senryu

a little boy
in an old man's body
second childhood

Senryu

silk stockings
smooth as baby's skin
wrinkled legs

Senryu

never know
if coming or going when
'round it goes

Haiku

God's angels
minister to the saved
one or a host

Senryu

telescope
eye at wrong end
paramedics

Senryu

what goes
around comes around
I've read

Senryu

portrait artist
always painting the ugly
will starve

Haiku

earth's canopy
as a changing canvas
God's eternal brush

Haiku

picture perfect
God's brush works perfection
His every stroke

Senryu

a horse of
different color
paint job

Haiku

full moon
howling of wolves
empty

Senryu

two armies
both in camouflage
fighting blind

Senryu

computer
assimilates information
virus

Senryu

piggy bank
takes deposits
shake ... shake

Senryu

removed
lashes and wig
for a start

Senryu

natural
at playing piano
daily practice

Senryu

a pretty tune
she sings like a bird
without words

Senryu

Labor Day?
in a year, one day
recognized

Put No Confidence in the Flesh

(Cinquain)

Lawyers
Integrity …
While questioned by many,
Are condemned many times in the …
Bible

Quiet Strength

(Cinquain)

Restful
Silence and peace,
The early morning hour,
Meditation on the Lord and …
Heaven

Renewed Heart

(Cinquain)

"Thou canst …
If Thou wilt! Oh,
Lord, that purges the heart;
Withhold not blessings that could …
Be mine."

Passing the Test

(Cinquain)

We want …
The Lord to hear
Us when we pray … He won't
If iniquity regarded …
In heart

We Ask and Receive Not

(Cinquain)

We pray …
With heart not right;
Ask the Lord for this or
That … while the Lord waits for us to …
Repent!

Power in Prayer

(Cinquain)

It's war …
Whom do we fight?
We pray to our great God!
He knows all the workings of the …
devil

Plunging into Hell

(Cinquain)

devil,
Always on hand …
In suicide missions
Deceiving them about God and …
Heaven!

More Than a Life

(Cinquain)

It's more
Than suicide
Mission ...taking one's life;
Plunges soul into Hell with the ...
devil!

Jabez' Prayer

(I Chron. 4: 9-10)

Jabez called on the God of Israel saying,
"Oh, that Thou wouldest bless me indeed and enlarge
My coast (borders), and that Thine Hand might be with
Me, and that Thou wouldest keep me from evil,
That is may not grieve me." And God granted him
                             that
                                 which
                                he
                                       requested!

Jabez, God is My God

(I Chron. 4: 9-10)
(Cinquain)

"Bless me …
Indeed, oh, God,
And enlarge my borders
Let Thine Hand be with me, keep me …
From evil"

Senryu

the preacher
announced no study
understatement

"Wild Green" Picking

(Triolet)

We went, "wild green" picking early today;
Much food grows wild, the Lord has put on earth:
Food good for man to eat … not just for hay;
We went, "wild green" picking early today;
Berries grow on vines, near the ground they lay;
Much nourishing food is found bound in the turf;
We went, "wild green" picking today;
Much food grows wild, the Lord has put on earth.

206

The "Salt Box" House

(Triolet)

The "Salt Box" house for 150 years has stood;
Large families with children lived in this place;
This age, each must have a room to live good!
The, "Salt Box" house for 150 years has stood;
Such tales of life told … if speak, the house could;
Three rooms for a family, means a small space;
The, "Salt Box" house for 150 years has stood;
Large families with children lived in this place.

On Hate

(Triolet)

Hate assuredly hurts the perpetrator,
Hate festers as a putrid sore inside;
At first, doesn't hurt as much as later;
Hate assuredly hurts the perpetrator,
The hated fares better than the hater;
Each answer to God … with self must abide!
Hate assuredly hurts the perpetrator,
Hate festers as a putrid sore inside.

Despondency

(Triolet)

The hole of despondency is enlarged;
Doubting … anyone can find himself there!
Many headlong into depression barge!
The hole of despondency is enlarged!
With lack of faith, God's children, will be charged:
The devil uses doubts … on all he dares!
The hole of despondency is enlarged!
Doubting … anyone can find himself there!

The Way to God is Through His Son

(Triolet)

One may call on God … yet, call in vain.
Without faith in Christ, God ... will not hear;
None other name by which men are saved,
One may call on God … yet, call in vain;
Thirteen times in ninety seconds … named …
Without Christ … hell-bound … the devil cheers;
One may call on God … yet, call in vain,
Without faith in Christ, God … will not hear.

The idea for this poem came from a newscast with Joe Leiberman.

Eclectic

Unusual

The nighttime was made for sleeping;
Off with shoes when going to bed!
With slumber "zzz's", the mind sweeping,
When clothes are changed, to rest the head.

The morning of the A.C.T. test!
Finds many eyes drooping with sleep;
Removing shoes to do their best???
Heard remarked … this would make scores leap!

Fifteen or twenty pair in a row;
Owners await signal to write …
Shoes all sizes … both high and low,
Improve test score? … they say, "that's right!"

Time runs out with the timer's "ding";
There's such a start midst the "sleepy" group,
Eyes open wide … seems dreams take wing;
Test in hand, but "out of the loop."

There's such a scramble at end of test,
Each determined to find his shoe …
Not finding their own … did their best!
One of a kind … there were quite a few!

Have You Ever? I Have

Have you ever been to church
   where the preacher failed to study? … I have!
And kept telling you he hadn't, all through the service? I
      have!
When, frankly seems he should have known,
   he needn't say a word … I have!
When it had to be obvious to all, whose time he took … I
      have!

God's call to the ministry …
   the highest calling … unto man;
Why answer God's call … then not prepare
   to study in advance!
The neglect of God's Word won't be excused
   again and again!
God does the calling … the message comes by prayer,
   study … not chance.

With one hundred people … listen for thirty minutes each
      of time …
That's fifty hours of time, to answer for,
   the preacher's taken;
Larger the congregation … more time taken,
   when all's combined.
No need to tell when there's no study…
   it won't be mistaken.

It's God's Word, the Holy Spirit, has promised
   to accompany …
The Bible states … God's Word …
   not singing, that will not return void;

When so called "singing" …
    takes precedence over Bible preaching –
The true meaning of worshipping God is …
    trampled and destroyed.

Have you been to church where the preacher failed
    to study? … I have!
Through his "message" this
    information … did continually weave …
When it had to be obvious to all,
    whose time he took … Have you ever? I have!

Level the Playing Field

Hey! Why are there twenty points on scoreboard?
It's thirty minutes before the game starts!
Oh, that's what, "Affirmative Action" affords;
Not fair … like putting horse behind the cart!

A tennis match starts at, "love" minus twenty;
That's IF players are of a different color …
Making God's work of color an enemy!
Political, "racket" – isn't folklore.

With baseball, there's such a variety of race …
Picked players would start the game with, "homeruns"
Scored … not batting, running or touching base;
Sports, soon nostalgia … with none lost or won!

The above asinine lines are insane!
Just leave it … play fair! Don't discuss further,
For the fans go to see a fairly played game;
A player or team vying with another.

On A.C.T. … S.A.T. excellence aimed…
Doing their best, in same time, with same test;
"Colorblind," the score is own, "gain" or, "blame,"
As answers, each from his own brain must wrest.

No points added in sports ... why, "game of life"?
Need, "play" by the rules, in school and workplace!
Ignoring higher grade points has been rife…
While adding points to unqualified base.

Supporters of "Affirmative Action" …
And those who benefit from the biased plan,
If applied to sports, humiliation … WON:
No games … unless fairly played, fans demand!

A "level playing field" … discrimination!
With jobs and schools, the same as if in game;
With God, there's no respecter of persons:
His Word teaches … we are to act the same.

Trusting in Christ … doing the best one can;
Not only, "sports" with practice to excel …
Same attitude in school will, "WIN" again!
Job or ring of school bell, "mettle" will tell.

Cats Kill Pests

Cats have helped man from ancient times,
Their eyes adjust to the night.
Killing rats and mice they find,
Eyes become slits when it's light.
Cats do most of their grooming,
Depend on others for needs.
Independent though … indeed!

I Was Thought of First!

My son …
When three; asked for
A mother just like me to…
Do the work, while we played … I'd have been
First cloned!

All Mouth

A tiny little bitsy flea;
That jumps so fast – it's hard to see;
First on my dogs …then next on me –;
Where is he … he lives so free …
Oh! What a bite … I know it's he;
He's, "all mouth" … I see, there's the key.

A Dumb Animal? – Who Said? Not I!

Have you ever noticed how happy your dog is to
   see you?
No matter if you're gone a short while or
   a longer spell …
When you return, such greeting … you receive –
   but, from another person – you never do!
We could all learn a lesson – demonstrating to
   those we love – yet, no words to tell.

Though your dog can't speak – love is manifest
   without doubt …;
Faithful and true … so happy always to see and
   be close to you –;
Are our dogs smarter than we – understanding
   what true love is about …
It behooves us to show affection, making effort – if we
   would the path of friendship and love pursue.

If you're happy when someone who's been away –
  returns …
Why not rejoice … thank God – they're safely back
  home –;
Many leave to never again return … for God is in
  control – we need to learn …
Yes – we all could learn a lesson from our own little dog
  who doesn't ask much – and is happy with a bone!

Good-bye Big Fish

"I got a big fish, but it's a mama –;"
So back it's thrown into the water …
Never keep the big ones unless for the wall –
Have enough of that – not a fish stall.

Quite a different "angle" for an angler;
Instead of "the big one got away …" a tangler …
Just keeping the small ones another tale;
Somewhere or other … wind blowing a gale.

My son who loves to fish, better than to eat;
Manages his own interpretation, never to be beat –;
He says the big ones don't taste so very good …
My answer to him … not knowing the whim –,
    "But, eat one I would!"

If the big ones … caught on his line …
Don't exceed what's on his wall … that defines –
Back into the water … its life prolonged;
He says that's sportsman ethics … "Good-bye fish – so
    long."

But, expectantly, he takes his boat and gear …
Hoping the big ones … let go another year;
Will take the bait … having gained in weight,
When he turned one loose…
     he figured on another encounter … a later date.

For my son, Ron

Losing Weight

You hear so much … about losing weight –
Dieting is a nuisance … if you wait too late;
Weight doesn't disappear … as if never near,
Attaches fast … in one big mass …;
Causing weight to soar – weighing more and more;
If you aren't careful – you'll weigh more than before.

You hear of the pictures –"before and after" –;
See many such … fat then slim …;
Pictures advertising … what to make thin;
All of this shown … then to defend…
Never see a picture – of what happened next –;
Bigger than before, in a little time– many indexed.

Takes willpower … to always eat right –;
Better health is a dividend of a good diet.
Besides looking nicer slim and trim –;
Feeling more like you did way back when –
Make it a habit to eat right each day –
Then, "I'm too fat" – You'll never, be heard to say!

The Mule

The mule is a stubborn thing,
As if stubbornness was its right.
A blind bridle gives a signal;
Stubbornness, we all, need fight.

Must we wear blind bridles, too?
To keep our eyes on the Lord …
That keeps us from looking back,
Losing all, if any, rewards.

People can have hearts the same,
Stubborn and rebellious, too …
As witchcraft and idolatry …
That Bible says what's true.

With stubbornness, what is gained?
Witchcraft and idolatry are evil …
God has never blessed these traits!
Witchcraft's not only medieval!

It's the mule's inherent nature;
He continues with the same heart
What he is, he'll ever be …
No change on his part.

God gave man the power of choice
Accept or reject His Son …
You can become like the mule,
Stubbornness, that's second to none.

Would you rather be a mule,
Following your own stubborn heart?
Bringing nothing but heartache …
Yielding to right's where to start.

The mule is a stubborn thing,
As if stubbornness was its right
A blind bridle is a signal …
Stubbornness, the Lord helps fight.

Thankless

"As thankless as a toothless child." … Scripture
      referring to a baby … teaching you and me;
A baby so lovable, dependent, demanding, thankless –
      for everything's taken for granted … all's for free.
Do we, as we grow into adulthood, continue
      to feel the same … as if life's only a game?
When we're old and gray, still accepting
      all God's blessings without being thankful … we're to
blame.
Take a look around … so many benefits furnished
      by God … what does one have to be, "thankless" about!
Many priceless blessings are bestowed upon saint as well
as   sinner…
                  no doubt.

Much taken for granted … by everyone … air we
      breathe … flowers, trees, water, sunshine … as well as the
            rain …
Just a few to name … for the just and unjust …
      benefiting the same –;
Shameful to neglect thankfulness … to a
      God Who loves us so …

He gave Jesus, His Son, for the salvation of our
    soul, … yet we treat Him not as a loving Father,
        but as a foe.
To be as "thankless as a toothless child" …
    means ingratitude; life will soon be gone …
If one has teeth … perhaps the ones now
    are not your own … thank you to the Lord
        is due … and best, by actions shown.

Camouflage

Camouflage is not always camouflage:
It can turn to be conspicuous;
Though hard to see in trees where one can dodge;
When brought to view, a sight that can disgust.

To camouflage, some terrain, help does lend,
Unseen in surroundings as if in kind …
All goes well if nature conspires to blend:
Camouflage, in wrong place, easy to find.

Personality can camouflage what's real …
Bad character … it covers, tries to seal;
If fraudulent, time will tell … truth won't kneel;
Threadbare, personality's curtain … reveals.

Things are not always as they seem to be;
Character is what a person really is …
Personality is what others only see!
That hidden is brought to light, not in disguise.

Others may for a time act as foliage;
Covering as does a forest of trees …

God looks into all hearts; that is His gauge!
Man born depraved, has a crippling disease.

Camouflage just won't work; God sees the heart;
He sent Christ to die for the sin of man …
Repentance with faith, is the place to start:
Salvation is through Christ, accept while you can.

"Be not deceived," we're told, "God is not mocked;
What a man sows, that shall he also reap" …
Christ, at the sinner's heart does stand and knock;
No camouflage, when Christ and sinner meet!

Hearts changed will no longer blend with the crowd;
A different lifestyle is seen to take place …
In prayer, with thanksgiving, knee and head bowed;
A lost sinner saved … covered by God's grace.

One Thing Calls For Another

One thing calls for another … a neverending
    ring –;
If there's music … we must have someone
    to sing –.
With the singing – everyone expects there to
    be music …;
When everything isn't as it should be all
    together … some are just sick.

Apple pie calls for cheddar cheese or ice
    cream …
To not have the two … is nothing less
    than mean –.
Hot dogs must have mustard and a
    relish …

Not to provide these spicy additions would
    be somewhat devilish.

Baseball could be played with regulation
    uniforms, but not without their caps –
A terrible tragedy if required to do so …
    what a mishap …
They couldn't take the cap off … twist
    and turn – fit it back just so – looking stern;
So much of the game … eccentricities –
    changing so fast – their code defying us learn.

These are just a few … they simply go together –
    else useless as a fireplace without wood …
Or as a letter without a stamp … which will
    never get where it should –;
If you'll think a little … life is so wrapped
    up – one thing or another waiting to trip us up;
Such small things – allowed too much to
    disrupt – even as we sit down to sup.

Something so important as values … escape
    much notice …
Neglected to practice or teach … therefore
    forfeiting much solace –;
The Bible teaches to train up a child in
    the way he should go…
Example and teaching cannot be separate
    and apart – parents either accept responsibility or woe!

All to Himself ...
Yet, Not Alone

As the fall sun shines on the tall grass;
With the dew still sparkling ... yet, drying fast;
The man doing the work ... has a big job to do;
Covering acre upon acre ... as the work he pursues.
As the tractor roars and rolls along;
Weeds and grass are mowed and gone.
Two deer jump in a thicket of green,
When a covey of quail ... flying away is seen.

The noise of the tractor obscures the birds' song;
Yet, when he stops to listen, birds are singing along.
Resting awhile ... he watches and listens for a spell;
Many different birds ... by their singing he can tell;
Starting the tractor to mow again;
Cutting, laying thick ... spreading like a fan.
As he drives his tractor ... looking over land;
He thinks of the many ways ... God has blessed so grand.

As he moves on ... continuing to mow ...
Across the field ... strip by strip, on he must go;
With the noise of the tractor, he hears no other sound;
Mind far away – thinking of Heavenly things, here not found.
He frequently thinks on his sermon while at work ...
Preaching so many years ... Scriptures in his mind, always
lurk.
His desire ... telling others of Christ, God's plan for man;
He studies and prays ... that those who hear will understand.

For Carl, my husband

Where My Money Went!

Where my money went – I'd like to know!
Thought I was keeping up – but away it went –
As if upon it, the wind did blow,
It seems I could own a mint;
At month's end, still run low,
Perhaps, even without a cent!

Trying to account where money did go;
So much disappears without a hint.
Sure it's right – I'm my biggest foe –
Much better if money to myself I lent;
Charged high interest – payment just so!!
Then I'd have money regularly like rent.

Just pay myself – as others I always do;
Never running late – to have a clear slate.
It's an honorable way of life to pursue.
If to myself – payments wouldn't be late!
Plenty of money – not bills in lieu!
What a thought; just be my own banker – to date!!

Would do better than most people think
If we'd treat ourselves as the bank.
We just sail along – 'till we've almost "sank";
Hmm! Could charge a penalty if we run late –
Never notice until bank account's lank!
No responsibility – we say it's just fate!!

Gems of Wisdom By Maxine

1. Charity begins at home ... many times we hear people say –
   Excuses won't heal a broken heart or the hungry feed. If we cared nothing for family our own ... there's no need for us to pray.

2. The messenger of death enters, and all business stops.

3. A good neighbor is a found treasure.

4. It is your own lantern ... do not poke holes in the paper which covers it.

5. Scattered forces defeat a general before he does battle.

6. Remember, fears, you must hold from you as you would avert a sword pointed to your throat, when you have a shield in your hand to raise between.

7. In times of great danger, one standing alone may be as a too lightly rooted tree facing a storm of wind.

8. The swiftest of horses cannot overtake a word once spoken.

9. Before you scold a dog, learn his master's – or his mistress' name.

10. Teachers open the door; you enter by yourself.

11. You have lingered nearly too long in the courts of childhood; it is time you walk into the future.

12. Let the storm rage, but just ride it out – then go about your own business.

Logging a Log

There are those who pride themselves,
Up-to-date with a daily log …
Into personal issues delve;
While "logging" … living in a fog!

God's word teaches that you do …
Unto others as you would
Have them to do unto you;
Each can do better and should!

There is an ALL-Seeing-Eye …
Recording thoughts and acts … true;
God knows ALL … no one denies,
Repent is what ALL … need do!

Account for each idle word …
Will be given in Judgment;
Words, depart … by many heard,
Heard by ALL who don't repent.

Names of ALL saved God has logged;
Keeping a record of ALL deeds …
Salvation through Christ is free,
Rewards require works … you see!

When a person does log book fill,
What good has the logging done …
God's record not rendered nil!
Repentance for … EVERYONE!

Those logging need know God's Son:
Angels do God's logging … still!

For ALL who are "hep" on logs!

227

Your Job and You

(Sonnet)

Everyone has a job ... always lots to do ... so many
    things you need pursue.
If you don't go to work each morning ... or
    sometimes even if you do –;
Things at home must be done, and there's
    no one to do it – but you!
While falling behind – seeing many things
    to remind;
Must be careful or get yourself – in an –
    awful stew.
Discouragement it seems ... comes, in, on
    a beam;
Finding fault with everything – just can't work
    fast enough ... time to redeem!
But, what if you didn't have a job ... or ...
    anything to do?
Then you would – no doubt – your plight –
    sit and rue!
Wouldn't you rather get up ... able to go to
    work;
Than be crippled and sick ... with no
    work to shirk?!!
Instead of complain, at your job of work, or
    at home, where a job ... always lurks;
Thank the Good Lord, you're able to maneuver –
    counting this as ... perks!!

Perspective's the Difference

Here we are again!
On a Saturday fine ...
With pencil in hand,
The answer behind.

A.C.T. Test day!
Sleep may rest in eyes ...
But, the best does lay,
In each heart to try.

Test-giver with ease,...
And in her own way;
Makes the test seem a breeze,
With drudgery at bay.

To make work seem play
Is always the best ...
Where, "dread" rules the day,
Everything seems a test!

Perspective's the thing:
Work and play are one;
On this verdict hangs,
When jury is done.

The difference between ...
Enjoyment's the proof:
Playing hard is seen
While work tires ... in truth!

God in His Wisdom,
Made people with choice;
Trust Him or complain ...
Complain or rejoice!

The Mouse

The mouse is so very small
Goes anyplace, slips under doors
Nibbles its way ... not by force
Scampers out, while the house snores.

Up one wall, down the other
Little field mouse moves about
In an instant changes route
Darting here and there, hiding.

Traps are set, poison put out;
Still, they thrive on what they find,
A few crumbs is all it takes!
Always mice! Just be resigned!

Where there are people, there'll be mice
Whether in barn or castle ...
They make their way, take their time
Instead of a few, a passel!

Lots of damage, a mouse can do!
Over time, it shreds and tears
Though timid it seems, is so fleet
Where one is seen ... there are pairs!

Mice must have sense of humor –!
Often lets himself be seen ...
In a room full of people
With his beady eyes agleam!

Upon table, women jump!
Screaming, screeching hysterically,
Guess they're more familiar with rats!
He's outnumbered numerically –!

The mouse is so very small
Goes anyplace, slips under doors
Nibbles its way ... not by force
Scampers out, while the cat snores!

Nostalgia

and

Romance

To Catch a Snowbird

Did you ever try to catch a snowbird?
When a child – it was such fun!
With snow all over – blowing wind could be heard;
No playing out today – to jump and run.
My daddy knew how to keep me entertained,
Staying in the house – I had to remain.

A window, to see the snow, but to go out, no use to beg.
Warm by the fire – my place I could pick.
My daddy would tie a string to a peg –;
Then the string through the windowsill was strung.
The peg propped the board – one end to the snow didn't
        stick.
Scooping out the snow under the board where it hung.

Corn sprinkled on the ground was the trick …,
To get the snowbirds under the board to peck.
Then pull the string – the board would fall – click!
Spending a lot of time like this – kept from being sick.
Never caught a snowbird … they were too quick –!
His plan worked fine, again! My activities to restrict!

*A Personal Note:
My brother, three sisters, and I still miss our parents so;
They always had something fun for us to do.
Both have gone on to meet the Lord many years ago.
We'll meet them again in Heaven, our lives made new.
If, for our children we do as good, defending from the foe;
As did our Mother and Daddy – only a few are as true!

Time Has Told

(Villanelle)

We met long … ago:
Near the village by the stream;
Love at first sight, we certainly know!

It seemed time … a determined foe:
None to gain by fair means;
We met long ago.

God His love bestowed:
Abundantly, it seems;
Love at first sight, we certainly know!

God's call to preach … he knows:
He's had to work … and preach;
We met long ago.

Blessed of God, and greatly so:
Four children saved … redeemed;
Love at first sight; we certainly know!

Together we're growing old:
Faith in God … eyes that still gleam;
We met long ago:
Love at first sight, we certainly know!

If It's True Love

(Triolet)

True love not contingent on circumstance:
It twines two hearts like tendrils of ivy!
True love desires another's life to enhance;
True love not contingent on circumstance:
Can flourish in obscure shack or elegance;
In poverty or wealth … ill health or lively;
True love not contingent on circumstance:
It twines two hearts like tendrils of ivy!

True Love

(Triolet)

Ah! Love at first sight!
We know can prove true.
After years of married life, love's imagery is bright.
Ah! Love at first sight!
True love will last through the darkest of nights.
But, would it take a chance if the troubles it knew?
Ah! Love at first sight!
Few know it can be true.

Remembering Where We Met

(Triolet)

I remember where we met;
Though it was long ago;
We met by the old village stream;
I remember where we met;
It seems like only yesterday my heart did fret;
And the short time together, a remembered foe;
I remember where we met;
Though it was long ago.

For: Carl

Without Price

(Sonnet)

True love proves true – whatever else to rue;
Mattering not the demand, to withstand –;
True love will not, be foolishly pursued;
Always it seeks … not knowing where to find;
As elusive as moonbeams, yet, strong as death;
Love's bonds continue wrapping hearts the more;
For time goes past this way once – keeping score.
All remedies, to change – what's been – folklore.
True love bears, over all obstacles – soar.
Love to be true … is only up to you …
Regardless if alone … some gone before;
True love exalted – has purity due …
Without price – yet labor freely given;
No recompense is sought – none to be bought.

"Better Than Sunday"

Sunday was my favorite day when just a girl,
    now, after all these years … remaining … still is.
At home, we always attended church … my own
    family does, too –;
The preacher most always stayed with
    us … making our home as his;
That was the way my Mother and Daddy
    and we five children wanted him to do.

He lived a long distance away … traveling to
    preach … then going back home.
He traveled by bus to his appointments –
    not only to our church he preached, but another plus.
From his home he spent much time …
    he was an older preacher – children all grown.
We all loved him – appreciated that for
    which he stood – just part of our family to us.

Sunday has always been my favorite day –
    a time for worshipping at our church –;
After the church service and spiritual
    food …
Home, then to a scrumptious Sunday lunch … with so
    many at times –
    one could hardly find a place to perch.
Such fellowship reflecting the love of
    God … everyone in a spiritual mood.

Sundays have been special all through
    the years …
And with God calling my husband to preach,
Sunday was always very busy with four
    children to care for.
My husband, being the preacher was kept
    quite busy – so being left with the four –
        I had to teach.

Sunday being as it is … a wonderful day …
Where God's people gather to worship and
    fellowship as one –;
"Yet, in Heaven, everyday will be better
    than any Sunday" … in every way;
All who accept Christ as Savior will live
    in Heaven eternally … where "everyday is better than
        Sunday" when life on earth is done.

New With the Old Versus Old With the New

If everyone who is married –
Would resolve to make a new start.
Let your interest together be varied.
Be considerate and honest – heart to heart!

Seems it would be the best –,
A new start with your own spouse.
Letting them know of your love – no guess.
Interest for both should be your own house.

There are times when only one is at fault,
God's word teaches one's untrue to the other –;
    when that occurs;
Even He sanctions the one bringing the
    marriage to a halt.
If not in accordance with God's teachings –
    defer.

Think on this – wouldn't it be better to make a
    new start –;
With the old than – to go through all involved,
And make an old start with the new?
If possible – with God's help – problems with,
    the first one resolve.

The Three "R's" and More

Getting there early … ringing the bell – to be heard
   over hill and dell …
The little white one-room school, already warm – heated
   by the big stove … before ringing of the bell –;
The school board member living close by … when it was
   needed – made his way, building the fire –;
On cold mornings, all warm and cozy – students arriving
   … unless circumstances dire.

The three "R's" … English, spelling, history …
   other subjects, too;
Filled the day … for teachers and students with plenty
   to do …
Getting the subjects for each class from first grade
   through eighth …
Worked around … not wasting time … for recesses – not
   wanting to be late.

Recess was "fun-time" for all … the teacher, not much
   older – joined in a game of ball –;
Though "Work-Up" was the chosen game … pitching always
   to the teacher did fall …
Her pitching left-handed … they thought fun and liked to see;
Pitching … her very best – striking some out … one
   two and three … "that" pitcher was ME.

Lots of fun times ... to look back upon and to always ...
   remember...
We practiced for our Christmas program – it was good
   we had until December !!!
Though the school was small ... each student played an
   important part ... never diminished.
Each doing his best ... encouraging the rest ... in all
   things – from start to finish.

My sentiments then ... the same as now ... no education
   is complete ... without a knowledge of God ...
That might not be politically correct ... or what some
   just call, "mod" –;
That was the way of it then ... missionaries ... monthly,
   did come ;
Prayer and Bible study were an integral part ... thinking
   one is educated without God's Word, is being dumb!!!

Back then, it seemed education was more appreciated ...
   and learning was fun –;
Each family was responsible for educating their own
   daughters and sons ...
It wasn't expected of the community or village "per se"
   to be responsible for all;
Yet, ALL ... were expected, and did care for their own ...
   many hardships, working together, didn't appall.

So much we hear about "back to basics" ... we've waited
   so long – pray this is the year;
Now it's all, "higher learning" ... yet, it makes the news
   about the "educated" not able to read ... we hear ...
In the one-room school, correct answers were the same ...;
   each student learned two plus two was four – to name –;
And reading was something they learned long before ...
   graduating through the door.

Poverty and Wealth

Poverty and wealth … only a part of the
   marriage vows;
To some it's of utmost importance, taking
   preeminence over all else.
Some never marry because – wanting finances
   just right – they're not having … make this remark!
So many – if things don't go just right …
   and their finances don't excel;
First to come to mind … just cancel out
   the affairs of the heart.
Having such high monetary hopes – when
   supposedly – in love they fell;
Wounding the other – who was trusting
   sincere and true at the start.
This type reasoning is common – from sea
   to sea – across hill and dell.
At the first financial trouble or – a decrease in the
   ol' bank account – they part.
But, with true love you'll find … poverty or
   wealth – no difference for love indwells.
Hardships – even poverty – strengthen true love –
   perhaps, all belongings on a cart.
If however, material things – mean more than
   someone to love … yourself – you'll soon repel.
God can bless a husband and wife –'till all –,
   on it will remark – financially as well!
God's blessing – of finding a true love – is from
   above – a bit of the Bells of Heaven – wedding bells!

Tell Me

"Tell me – tell me true – tell me you love me in
    January when snowflakes fall – snowbirds call – tell me
        you love me –.
In February – tell me, too … you love me –
    when cold winds blow – Feb. 14th – you love me forever
        … so!
March – you must not forget the need to tell
    me, too – you love me – love me … you really do …
April, when the showers come – tell me you love
    me – love me – do – as refreshing as the dew.

In May, come the flowers after the April showers –
    you love me – I love you – I really do …
It's June – the month of weddings – tell me
    you love me – love me truly – even with a tear …
July comes with the hot summer sun … a summer
    night's moon – we're in love – you tell me – I tell you –;
August, with summer almost over … don't forget
    to tell me – "I love you – love you truly, Dear."

September … summer gone … but love is
    strong … don't forget to tell me you love me – the yearlong…
October is fall at its best – not too cold to live
    with zest – tell me your love me – love me best …
November …the ending of the fall – the night
    bird's call – if you love me – let me hear –;
December – the beginning of winter – wind from the
    north, east and west – tell me you love me … I will rest!"

Home

and

Family

Welcome!

A refreshing word … welcome … you're always
   welcome … come when you can …
We so long to see you … time short or long …
   nothing to withstand –;
Much preparation needed to get everything organized
   and ready;
With anticipation of your visit … all things
   are heady …
Wishing you lived closer, and didn't have to come
   from so very far away –;
Knowing the distance you travel makes for a
   shorter stay …
Thanking you for your love and concern … to come
   for a visit – dear to our heart;
Always remembering the good times, and love we all
   shared from the start.

Welcome!! … it's home … welcome you always will
   ever be;
Though you have your own home now… the same
   as we –;
There's still a part … to always be remembered
   of the past …
That you never will forget … while you have breath
   'till your very last;
Home … the place you grew up … from a child so
   very young …
Always to remember the home around where memories
   as gossamer are hung –;
Reminiscing of the fun … yet, values where Jesus
   was always number one …
Never forgetting the training in family devotionals
   at setting of the sun.

Welcome ... that's the way it always should be,
    Whether I visit you or you visit me –;
Our hearts entwined in a lasting love ... yet, at all
    times free ...
Never forgetting our parents and home ... midst life's
    turmoil and strife;
Taking time to visit parents and the old home place
    from your busy way of life –;
Honors God and parents ... God commands you honor
    them.
A family centered around God's love and Holy Word
    is pleasing to Him.
Parents should be thankful if children ... though
    busy ... still want to come home;
To fellowship ... as in the past ... not leaving aging
    parents ... hearts barren and so alone.

Welcome! The homecoming in Heaven when Jesus with
    our loved ones we see;
No more short earthly visits ... for all who have been
    saved ... there'll be –;
Eternity to bask in the eternal sunshine of God's
    matchless love –;
But, only those who have made preparation while here
    below, for that life above;
God gave His only begotten Son ... Christ must be the
    choice ... best not delayed;
With the choosing of Christ as Saviour ... Salvation
    grows sweeter ... never fades ...
Hearing WELCOME to a whole family in Heaven ... will
    show, while on earth, preparations were made.
No more partings ever ... so thankful am I that
    welcome won't by our, "frail abilities" be gauged.

Some Remain

There remain those, to whom family grows ever,
   more dear …
Values taught them in growing up … not only ears,
   but, hearts, did hear –;
Never forgetting the closeness to father and
   mother and siblings while growing up;
Back in time when the whole family was home
   to sit down to sup.

None of this modern day … of running here, there,
   to and fro …,
Time was spent together … to work, though did have
   to go –,
Home was an important place … whether large or just
   a little space, to children, husband and wife;
And regular worship in Church together …was a
   way of life.

Holidays were enjoyed by the grandparents, uncles,
   aunts, nieces, nephews, … the whole family …
Birthdays, Thanksgiving, Christmas … all others,
   just any –;
A time for celebration, and to enjoy games and
   family fun;
Picnics and outings … where everyone was so tired
   at setting of the sun, when day was done.

Family closeness … like anything worthwhile needs
   be cultivated to be …
Each sharing, caring, working, loving … doing their
   best to see …

That the others have the love, care and attention
    that's needed;
All for one … one for all … remains paramount and
    always determinedly heeded.

No matter what age … everyone important … each had
    a part …
Family gatherings never complete … until the last
    one there to start –;
Responsibilities were taught … so all could learn,
    no matter the age;
With faith in the Lord … taught of His Word …
    preparation for the world outside … had to be
        the gauge.

All Not Said or Done

Vacation for some, means work for others:
To have everything ready when they come;
Many extra things you try to get done …
So there'll be time for all to have some fun;
Preparing ahead what dishes you can …
Remember the vacation … you make again!
Family has grown, and to forget you're prone;
They've grown older, but not just them alone.

A few days isn't long for a visit …
Especially when having to come so far;
The ones coming are worn … children so tired;
Those making ready at home, nothing hired;
Both traveler and host are not at their best:

But, have a good visit ... forget the rest ...
The few days managed will be gone once more –
Advise ... enjoy what's good ... the rest ignore.

You must have done a few things, which were right,
For them to arrive with eyes shining bright ...
Coming to spend a while at their old home –
No matter where on earth they live or roam;
Trying to catch upon all that that is past ...
All the new's-interesting ...   subjects are vast;
The Lord's blessings will be discussed and told;
Causing faith to be increased ... doubts to fold.

Though work and travel worn ... all will admit;
Thanking the Lord ... for allowing the visit.

What's a Birthday?

A birthday means – one year older, but a lot
of other things;
Love and laughter ... cake and gifts ... from
candy to rings.
The way of celebrating changes as the years
go by;
It seems the older one gets ... the faster the
years fly.

Baby's first birthday is always so important
to everyone else but baby ...
However, the cake and ice cream will vanish
quickly ... left to himself;

Birthday cake, the icing and cream, all over
the place – face and hands …
All this will change … as the hourglass of
time disperses its sands.

Next, … all dressed up to party with friends –
who help celebrate the day;
Too much of a good thing … cake and ice cream,
candy and things, with a "tummy ache" pay;
Birthdays are exciting and another thing to
thank the Lord for …
A birthday's only by His grace … it could as
easily … be … or … nor.

Big parties, little parties … or party … none
at all …
The years do add … as one by one the birthdays
fall;
Three score and ten … the Bible says, is man's
allotted time;
And they're labor and sorrow if by reason of
strength … they're eighty … combined.

It's appointed unto man once to die and after
this the judgment …
Must accept Christ as Saviour during time to
you the Lord has lent –;
He came that we might have life and have it
more abundantly;
With Him beside us, we can be free … though,
"birthday" years … do flee.

Each birthday is special to one's self ... and to
    many others ...
Celebrating our own or partaking in the ...
    celebration ... helping in another's;
Not for years ... but, as we older grow ... to −
    appreciate the years and good health we're led.
Each of us know ...with our heart, not just our ...
    head, before the next birthday, we could be dead.

Children Pay

(Hosea 4:6)

In time's past, God has destroyed his people,
For lack of knowledge ... God rejected them;
Since thou hast forgotten the law of God,
God told them He would forget their children.

Children are a heritage of the Lord ...
They're not ours; they're only on loan from God:
Teaching children right brings its own reward;
Bible teaching of discipline not mod!

We're to train a child in the way he should go,
When he's old, he will not depart from it.
Loving parents ... to many things say, "no"...
Teaching trust in Christ, their sins to remit.

Charity and Home

Charity begins at home – so many times we
    hear them say –
Excuses won't fill the cup or the hungry feed.
If we care nothing for our own – there's
    no need for us to pray.
We're worse than an infidel in the Bible
    we can read …
Better be kind at home – than pretending to worship,
    burning incense far away.
Then neglect to provide – for those God
    has given us … with deeds.

Shadow

Mother and Dad believed our pets were a part of our family. Once we had a pet, it was ours for life, so we thought it befitting to close this volume with a poem about Mother's little Schipperke dog she had for over fourteen years. (See the picture of Maxine and Shadow)

When you mention shadow,
What do you immediately see?
No doubt, it's to represent faintly,
A picture of you or me.
Staying close as can be – seen vaguely;
Darting here, there – but, never free.

Shadow is more than that you know.
Would you believe loyal, true, unconditional love?
Racy and fast, but a heart shot as with cupid's bow;
Gaining such love is a treasure trove.
Always protective from friend or foe,
You feel secure as resting in a cove.

Shadow, if you haven't guessed,
Very special – I could write a log.
One lesson all to learn – as friend, the very best,
When it comes to her, I'm in no fog.
So many times – stood the friendship test;
My loveable, sharp, little black, Schipperke dog!